CREATIVE DANCE IN THE PRIMARY SCHOOL

CREATIVE DANCE IN THE PRIMARY SCHOOL

by

Joan Russell

Principal Lecturer in Dance
Worcester College of Education

MACDONALD & EVANS LTD.

8 John Street, London W.C.1

1965

First Published September, 1965
Reprinted February, 1966
Reprinted August, 1966
Reprinted July, 1967
Reprinted October, 1967
Reprinted July, 1968
Reprinted January, 1969
Reprinted August, 1970

©
MACDONALD & EVANS LTD
1965

S.B.N.: 7121 0316 3

To the memory of
Roland and Mercedes Russell

Printed in Great Britain by
UNWIN BROTHERS LIMITED
WOKING AND LONDON
(HL4022)

Preface

Creative Dance in the Primary School has been written in response to many requests for more detailed help for students and teachers concerned with the teaching of dance in the primary school. The analysis in Chapter 2 and the suggestion of its use as a basis for lesson planning in Chapter 4 have been found helpful to teachers attending short courses organised by a number of Local Education Authorities, in particular Berkshire, during the years 1959–64.

This book extends the details, given in *Modern Dance in Education*, of material found suitable for the various age groups from five to eleven years and these are based upon personal experience of teaching dance in several primary schools. Methods of presentation and the links with the other arts are also discussed. An important feature of this book is the inclusion of a number of photographs of children dancing. The purpose of this is to give some illustration of the suggestions made in Chapter 3 for the structure of the syllabus. One school was selected for the final experimentation with all the age groups. Although some of the children had previous experience of broadcast lessons in the "Music and Movement" series, they had limited experience in creative dance before this experiment. However, what must be emphasised, is that the children's achievements reflect not only the response to creative dance experience but also the climate within the school. Here the children were encouraged to become deeply involved in their own creative work covering many aspects and, because of this, made speedy progress in dance.

It is recognised that the quality of some of the illustrations may leave something to be desired, but it was considered important that the actual photography did not make the children self-conscious or camera-shy. For this reason special lighting was not employed and the camera used was as unobtrusive as possible. The photographs included were carefully selected from the hundreds actually taken because it was considered that their movement content far outweighed any imperfections.

J. R.

August 1965

Acknowledgments

THE scheme of work suggested owes much to discussions with colleagues engaged in exploring the content of the syllabus for Primary Schools at a conference of the Modern Educational Dance Section of the Association of Teachers in Colleges and Departments of Education held in 1961. I should like to thank especially Mr. E. Chapman, the headmaster of The Grove County Primary School, Malvern, and the members of his staff who co-operated so generously to enable me to try out this scheme throughout the school. I am indebted to my colleague Miss Brenda Sheridan for her help in carrying out the experiments with the children. I am also grateful to Mr. McKinlay, the headmaster of Henwick Grove Primary School, for allowing me to teach in his school.

My thanks are due to the following for permission to quote extracts from books: Random House Inc. for the extract from *Childhood and Adolescence* by Stone and Church; Routledge and Kegan Paul for the extract from *Rosegarden and Labyrinth* by Seonaid M. Robertson; Dennis Dobson for the extract from *A Commonwealth of Art* by Curt Sachs; Faber and Faber for the extract from *Education through Art* by Herbert Read; Harvard University Press for the extract from *The Process of Education* by Jerome S. Bruner; John Murray and E. P. Dutton, New York for the extract from *Wai-Wai* by Nicholas Guppy; to the Director of the Royal Scottish Museum for the extract from *Music and Dance in Indian Art*; to *The Observer* for the extracts from reviews by Christopher Wordsworth and Edmund Tracey; to the *Daily Telegraph* for the extract from the review by Donald Mitchell; to the editors of *Flourish* for the extract from that magazine; to the Physical Education Association of Great Britain and Northern Ireland for extracts from articles already contributed to their publications; to Miss L. Ullmann for the extract from the article "Symbol" by Rudolf Laban; and to Miss Celia Bishopp for her description of her work with children included in Chapter 6. My grateful thanks are due to the photographer, Mr. Geoffrey Hopcraft, for the skill and patience with which he overcame the limitations imposed upon him. The originals for Plates 2, 32 and 46 were kindly supplied by Mr. E. J. Wenham.   J. R.

7

Contents

Chapter

Preface 5

Acknowledgments 7

1. The place of dance in the primary school . . 11

2. Thinking in terms of movement: an analysis . . 19
   The body
   Effort: how the body moves
   Space and shape: where the body moves
   Relationship

3. The structure of the syllabus 31
   Infants and juniors: a suggested syllabus
   Stage 1: infants
       Infants, 1st year: material to be covered
       Infants, 2nd year: additional material
   Stage 2: juniors
       Juniors, 1st year, aged 7–8
       Juniors, 2nd year, aged 8–9
       Juniors, 3rd year, aged 9–10
       Juniors, 4th year, aged 10–11

4. The structure of the lesson 43
   A suggested plan
       Infants (reception class)
       Top infants
       Juniors 8–9 years
       Juniors 10–11 years
   Asking the right questions

5. Dance in relation to the other arts 51

6. Dance as a creative activity 60

Index 67

CHAPTER 1

The Place of Dance in the Primary School

WHEN we consider the scope for movement experience provided for children in school we see that it includes such activities as the P.E. lesson, games, athletics, swimming, outdoor pursuits and dance and drama. In all of these, except the last two, the main concern is with functional movement, that is, with body management and with mastery of the body in order to meet a variety of practical challenges. In dance and drama the main concern is with expressive movement, that is, with the mastery of the body in order to use the language of movement expressively and creatively. Dance and drama are expressive of the inner life, involving feeling and mood.

The fact is that when we carry out either functional or expressive activities we use bodily action. These two activities with common roots of liveliness in body and mind were frequently referred to by Laban as "doing" and "dancing." He suggests that while "doing" is purposeful and preserves life, "dancing" is necessary to recover from the strain of "doing" and as the primary means of expression from which the arts originate.

Dance has had many aspects during its long history since the primitive rituals and incantations to the gods. Among them are the stylised court dances, the folk dances of Europe, the delicate hand dances of the East, as well as contemporary social dances. These are hardly appropriate to the primary school, for the teaching of historical and folk dances would involve the child in memorising the set steps and patterns of social dances properly belonging to the adult world. This would be quite unsuitable.

It is as a contribution to the aesthetic and creative aspect of education that dance has a place. This implies that the child must be given opportunities to experience dance which grows directly from his personal movement expression. There is abundant evidence of his love of movement in his spontaneous jumping and hopping, his spinning and whirling, his dashing to and fro. Such rhythmic activity may indeed be the human being's response to the dynamic forces of life and the universe. If the child is to be helped to respond intensely and creatively through dance, the poetry of movement, the teacher must therefore study and understand movement.

We live in an environment full of movement. It is a manifestation of life itself and one way in which we can learn to understand the world is through our own sense of touch and movement. We observe growth in plant life. We distinguish the particular characteristics in animals which make typical, for example, the stalking of a cat, the hovering of a kestrel, the scurrying of a mouse. Even in apparent stillness there is much movement in the body—the beat of the heart, the contraction and expansion of the lungs and the nerve impulses coursing through to the brain. In human beings we observe an even greater range of movement possibilities than in other life forms.

Movement is one of the first means of expression, of communication and of learning about the world. The baby squirms, wriggles and kicks; he grasps and manipulates; he rolls, achieves a sitting posture and finally stands. So he grows and develops into a toddler who investigates everything in a most active way. He is rarely still. He pulls himself on to his feet, he clambers, scrambles and crawls. His hands are busy exploring and he learns about his environment through such activities as tasting, sucking, poking, prodding, tugging, pushing, pounding, tearing and generally manipulating.

Another reason for considering movement as a fundamental means of expression is that we have recourse to it when experience touches us deeply. We may clutch hold of someone in joy or fear, we slump in dejection, we rock and hug ourselves in despair, we gesticulate wildly in anger. We may even say "I'm speechless" or we may use ideas full of movement to express our feelings. Thus we say "I'm walking on air," "My hair stood on end," "I had a sinking feeling," "My heart leapt."

The young child shows his feelings immediately and spontaneously through his movement. His joy, his anger, his sulkiness can all be observed in his posture and gesture. Fairly soon, often too soon, he is expected to control and to hide these visible signs of his feelings.

Not only do we see movement as a primary means of expression but also we find it a basis of other forms of expression. In the field of speech we use different movements of the mouth to say "clitter-clatter," "O-oh," "tut-tut" or "slippery slithery slopes," and the words themselves conjure up a feeling of the experience so described.

The field of drama presents us with other examples. In connection with his playing of the parts of Prince Hal and Richard III at Stratford-upon-Avon in 1964, the actor Ian Holm has been reported as saying:

> "Richard III was much more vitriolic. I found myself going after effects that were jarring and abrupt—dynamic changes of pace and pitch, sudden sharp lunges of VOLUME [fortissimo]. Prince Hal is more of a piece: the character gets angry, of course, but the transitions are much smoother and continuous, nothing like the violent rage of Richard III."

In playing instruments we see different movements employed to create a rich variety of sound. Hands playing a drum can tap sharply, beat firmly, brush lightly, pound rhythmically. On a different level the movements of the conductor himself communicate his intentions to the orchestra. They may even go further. In writing of Colin Davis and Karl Böhm, whom he describes as "physical" conductors, Edmund Tracey* says:

> "Their gestures have such urgent eloquence that sometimes they seem to be drawing the shape of the music in the air: you can tell what the next bar is going to be like just by looking at them."

In painting his picture the artist will vary his touch, producing at times bold strong strokes, at others curved flowing lines and at others a light dabbing texture. The sculptor too will need to use a variety of movements in his hands as he manipulates his material. It was interesting to hear from a colleague who wanted to give freer expression in oils that exciting, lively pictures resulted once she suggested that students discard brushes and use their fingers and thumbs directly on the canvas. Seonaid Robertson,† taking this release even further, describes how she encourages the use of the kinaesthetic, rather than reliance on the visual sense, by working with

* *The Observer*, 19th January 1964.
† *Rosegarden and Labyrinth* (Routledge and Kegan Paul Ltd).

13

clay blindfold and by prefacing painting and modelling with movement experience. In this connection she describes preparations for the painting of a waterfall:

"I suggested to the children that if they wished they might close their eyes but in any case they should feel the movement of the water in their arms and their bodies. With the candle held in their hands, they first swung themselves into making the movement in the air, then, when they felt they had captured some water rhythm, without a break they transferred it to the paper with the candle wax which left (at this stage) no obvious trace."

She describes how when paint was added the candle grease marks were revealed, and concludes:

"So the movement which had been *felt* a moment before as an inner personal thing, miraculously became *visible* as something leaving its pattern on the world outside. These pictures had a directness and spontaneity which delighted them as much as me."

Movement then is manifest both as a means of expression in itself and as a vehicle of expression in other arts. It follows that scope is needed in the curriculum for the development of this aspect, and movement experience should not be limited to the functional activities only.

What is our deeper purpose in including the art of movement, and in particular dance, in the school programme? And is it worthy of a place in the curriculum?

A considerable amount of research is being carried out at present as to the nature of school experience, the content of the curriculum and on the learning process. In his book *The Process of Education* Jerome S. Bruner, Professor of Psychology at Harvard University, has summarised current thinking on new educational methods, particularly in science. He has set out his views on the conclusions reached by leading scholars and educators and has outlined a philosophy of education which provides an interesting challenge and yardstick against which to set the claims of any subject for inclusion in the curriculum. He suggests that the test is whether, when fully developed, it is worth an adult knowing, and whether having known it as a child makes a person a better adult.

Dance takes its place in the school curriculum because it satisfies this test. Ample evidence can be adduced from the stimulating creative work produced by children and students who have achieved sufficient mastery to create their own dance compositions.

Many of the ideas of such a group of educators coincide with and indeed reinforce the views and the approach of Laban.

The themes discussed by Bruner included the role of structure in learning, readiness for learning, the nature of intuition and the desire to learn. In considering the role of structure it is contended that effective learning occurs when emphasis is given to the learning of fundamental ideas which are then used as bases upon which to develop different aspects of those fundamental ideas. This type of learning, non-specific transfer or transfer of principles and attitudes, depends upon mastery of the structure of the subject matter:

"Grasping the structure of a subject is understanding it in a way that permits many other things to be related to it meaningfully. To learn structure, in short, is to learn how things are related."

It appears that it is not only necessary for children to grasp fundamentals early but also that the learning process is aided by developing an attitude of enquiry and a sense of excitement in discovery.

Another theme developed is that of readiness for learning. It is maintained that the foundations of any subject can be taught to anybody at any age in some intellectually honest form and that basic ideas are "as simple as they are powerful."

"To be in command of these basic ideas, to use them effectively, requires a continual deepening of one's understanding of them that comes from learning to use them in progressively more complex forms."

In discussing the nature of intuition a plea is made for a greater recognition of the importance of intuitive thinking, which is considered to be an essential, but often neglected, factor in the learning process and indeed in everyday life:

"As likely as not, courageous taste rests upon confidence in one's intuitions about what is moving, what is beautiful, what is tawdry. In a culture such as ours, where there is so much pressure towards uniformity of taste through our mass media of communication, so much fear of idiosyncratic style, indeed a certain suspicion of the idea of style altogether, it becomes the more important to maintain confident intuition in the realms of literature and the arts."

In dealing with the theme of motives for learning, it was stressed that the main need was that the material itself should be the best stimulus for learning, that the sense of discovery should be aroused and maintained. In particular much support must be given to humanistic learning as a corrective to the risk of over-emphasis on technology which is attendant upon the present situation.

It was with these very considerations that Laban was concerned. It was his work which helped us to appreciate that movement is fundamental in all life and that in man's efforts, whether functional or expressive, whether in work or in recreation, whether in large movements of the whole body or small unconscious movements of parts, there can be found common factors and fundamental principles. He helped us to look at human movement with new eyes: to observe more specifically, to analyse what we saw in terms of bodily action. So we have cause to appreciate that through the rhythms and patterns of an individual's movement his inner life is revealed and expressed. It is in the human being himself that the source of the material is found. As Laban wrote in the introduction to the sixteen movement-themes in *Modern Educational Dance* :*

"Each of the basic movement-themes represents a movement idea corresponding to a stage in the progressive unfolding of the feel of movement in the growing child, and in later stages to the development of his mental understanding of the principles involved.

"Each basic movement-theme contains many possible variations. Some themes or their variations can be combined with each other; others may be joined with one another through transmutations of their details."

His suggestions of themes suitable to form the basis of a scheme of work

* Rudolf Laban, Modern Educational Dance (Macdonald & Evans Ltd).

for use in school makes evident the interrelation of whole and part so that the structure of the subject is grasped at an early stage.

The dance lesson is not a time for rhythmic exercises to music nor for the performance of choreographed dances but a time for creative activity, as Laban infers:

"In schools where art education is fostered, it is not artistic perfection or the creation and performance of sensational dances which is aimed at, but the beneficial effect of the creative activity of dancing upon the personality of the pupil."

The lesson should aim to provide opportunities for the child to develop an understanding of his own movement capacities, to learn the language of movement and so invent and create sequences and dances of his own. In contrast to the teaching of set styles, where the direct method is used exclusively, the expressive aspect of movement is the main concern. As in Mathematics, Science, English and Art we want the child to discover, to explore and to use his imagination. We are concerned with the personal aspect, the involvement of the individual even at a simple level. We are not concerned with teacher-dominated work. The important thing is that the child is making something for himself. The result may be only a simple invention or a variation on a given theme but, as with his picture, his essay, his scientific experiment, it must be his.

We are not concerned with training dancers, with producing a skilled technical performance, nor are we concerned with developing a set style. We are concerned with educating through movement, with fostering the child's love of movement and with giving scope for discovery, imagination and intuition.

In thinking about the results to be achieved it is well to remember that the concern is with child art and with the learning process. In education in the visual arts the aims are to give the child opportunities to develop his sense of colour, line, form and texture, and gradually through his own experience to develop an awareness and an understanding of, and sensitivity towards, the principles underlying these artistic activities. So it is in the art of movement. We are not interested in teaching the child dances but in giving him opportunities to develop an increasing awareness of his bodily capacities and of his personal mastery of movement. To quote Laban:

> "The cultivation of artistic taste and discrimination in general cannot be furthered better or more simply than by the art of movement. Yet the dances which are produced must never originate from the wish to create outstanding works of art. Should such a miracle occur once, everybody will be pleased, but in schools we should not attempt to produce external success through effective performances."

Although a teacher may be particularly interested in one aspect or another of the arts, it is the sense of unity and interrelation which can be so exciting to teacher and child. Perceived as it is in so many ways—by eye, by ear, by the kinaesthetic sense itself—movement may be regarded as an integrating factor of major significance. We see, we hear and we feel movement. We see and feel shape and texture in angular, spiky, linear, curved, spiralled, rounded, rough, smooth forms. We recognise movement in sound—in legato, staccato, rhythm, accent, crescendo, diminuendo. We appreciate a sense of movement when we hear such words as soaring, surging, flying, swaying, circling, penetrating, growing. We can appreciate movement within a dramatic situation. For example, the meeting of the witches in *Macbeth* immediately suggests posture, body shapes, relationships, dynamics and action.

In the primary school we should aim to increase the child's power of observation and his sensitive awareness to movement, sound, shape, texture and rhythm.

Experience of the world of movement, of flying through the air, beating fast against the ground, spinning and whirling, carving pathways through the space, moving with care, with abandon, with haste, with leisure, with more tension, with less tension—all this, and more besides, is yet another aspect of the way in which we come to grips with the universe and with that fundamental manifestation of life and living matter which is movement.

CHAPTER 2

Thinking in terms of Movement: An Analysis

IF we wish to study movement then, we must observe human beings in action. Whether observing a child at play, a man's everyday or working actions, a skilled performer or a dancer, we can make an analysis of the movement under certain headings. In fact we tend to observe the unified whole, but by specific observation of one aspect or another a detailed analysis can be made.

The four main headings under which we observe movement are:

1. The body
2. Effort
3. Space and shape
4. Relationship.

If we take each of these in turn we shall be able to discover a number of interesting factors under each heading. In order to appreciate the validity of this analysis it would be best for the reader to observe a number of people, children or adults, in action in a variety of situations and so become aware of these various factors.

The body

This one might think of as the *structure* with which the activity is performed, the body being the *instrument* of expression. Thus we differentiate:

I. BODY ACTIVITY

We can observe what *activity* is being performed. This may be:

(a) *Locomotion* of some kind—for example stepping, running, rolling— with the intention of travelling along the surface of the floor in some way.

(b) *Elevation*—hopping, skipping, leaping, jumping, using the five basic possibilities of jumping—from one foot to the same foot; from one foot to

19

the other; from both to both; from both to one and from one to both—travelling upwards with the intention of leaving the floor and flying up into or through the air.

(c) *Turns*—spinning, pivoting, spiralling, whirling around, with the intention of constantly changing front.

(d) *Gesture*—shaping movements in the air with the arms or legs, gathering, scattering and penetrating the space.

(e) *Rising and sinking*—the rising action has the intention of reaching upwards, of striving for the greatest possible distance of one's body from the ground, pulling against gravity. The sinking action goes with the pull of gravity as the body drops, sinks, collapses, presses itself into the ground.

(f) *Opening and closing*—in opening there is the intention of broadening the body, reaching with the arms and legs to their own side and so stressing the openness and width in the body.

In closing there is a contraction, a folding, as the limbs reach across the body and arrive in a situation where all parts of the body are near to each other.

(g) *Advancing and retreating*—in advancing, the body reaches forward, using gestures of the arms with the intention of moving onwards. In retreating there is a drawing backwards with the intention of withdrawal.

2. BODY PARTS

We can observe which *parts* of the body are actively involved in the movement. These may be shown diagrammatically, as illustrated (p. 21).

We may observe whether the movement takes place in the body as a whole, as in travelling, flying or falling, or whether it takes place in particular areas or joints, as in the knees or arms or head. We can pay attention to what the less active body parts are doing—remaining relatively inactive, echoing the main movements, working in opposition.

3. BODY SYMMETRY

We can observe the *symmetry* or *asymmetry* of the body—whether both sides are moving similarly or one side is particularly emphasised by, for example, a gesture of arm or leg, or a drop or a lift of the side. A symmetrical shape is more stable, secure and calm, an asymmetric one is mobile, exciting and stimulating.

4. BODY FLOW

We can observe the *flow* of movement in the body and note whether it is simultaneous or successive. In simultaneous movement the action occurs in all the joints and body parts at the same time. In successive movement the action flows through from one joint and part to another and then another, e.g. shoulder, elbow, wrist, hand.

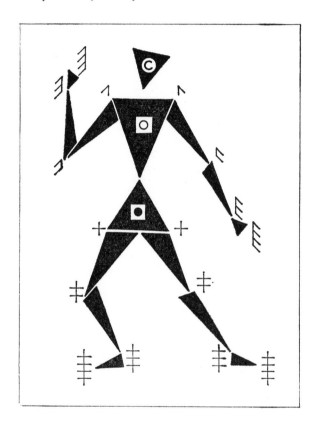

5. BODY SHAPE

We can observe the *shape* of the body as it crystallises in stillness. These shapes may be categorised as:

  (a) *Arrow-like:* one-dimensional: in a single direction or stress.
  (b) *Wall-like:* two-dimensional: with height and depth.
  (c) *Ball-like:* three dimensional: of curved and rounded nature.
  (d) *Screw-like:* three-dimensional: of twisted nature.

Effort: how the body moves

Here we are concerned with the attitude of the mover to the motion factors of weight, time, space and flow.

I. WEIGHT

We can observe the use of *weight* in an action. This may be *either* firm, strong, gripped, weighty *or* fine touch, delicate, light, airborne, buoyant.

2. TIME

We can observe the *time* taken in an action. This may be *either* sudden, quick, hasty, hurried, momentary, of short duration *or* sustained, slow, leisurely, unhurried, prolonged, of long duration.

3. SPACE

We can observe the *space pathway* followed in an action. This may be *either* direct, straight, undeviating, threadlike, of unilateral extension *or* flexible, wavy, roundabout, plastic, pliant, of multilateral extension.

4. FLOW

We can observe the *flow* of the action. This may be *either* bound, controlled, readily stopped *or* free, fluent, streaming onwards, abandoned.

Compounds of a quality of weight with one of time and one of space were termed by Laban *basic effort actions* and are set out as follows to show their relationship.

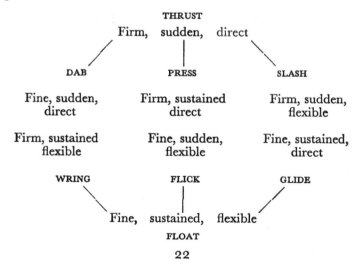

Space and shape: where the body moves

Here we are concerned with the shaping of the movement in the space.

1. EXTENSION

We can observe the *size* of a movement, which may be

(a) Small (near to the body), or

(b) Large (far from the body),

or degrees between.

2. LEVEL

We may observe the *level* into which the movement travels. This may be

(a) High.

(b) Medium.

(c) Deep.

When considering the whole body in action, *high* level refers to the area above the shoulder girdle. This is most naturally used by the arms and it is penetrated in leaping and jumping. The *deep* level refers to the area below the hips. This is most naturally used by the legs and is entered in crouching, sitting, kneeling, and lying. The *medium* level refers to the area between shoulders and hips which is most naturally used in turning.

3. DIRECTION

We may observe the *direction* towards which the movement travels. Certain directions will be penetrated as a result of particular activities. Thus rising and sinking will travel towards high and deep, opening and closing will travel towards the right and left sides, advancing and retreating will travel towards forward and backward (see page 20).

More complex activities will travel towards other directions. A movement, with the right side leading, which simultaneously rises and opens will lead into the direction high-right, while a counter movement which sinks and closes will lead into deep-left; one which sinks and opens will lead into the direction deep-right, while a counter movement which rises and closes will lead into high-left. The peripheral, circular pathway which links these four points of orientation, high-right, deep-right, deep-left and high-left, has been referred to as "the door plane." A movement, with the right side leading, which simultaneously opens and advances will lead into the

23

direction right-forward, while a counter movement which closes and re-treats will lead into left-backward; one which opens and retreats will lead into the direction right-backward, while a counter movement which closes and advances will lead into left-forward. The peripheral, circular pathway which links these four points of orientation, right-forward, right-backward, left-backward and left-forward, has been referred to as "the table plane." A movement which simultaneously advances and sinks will lead into the direction forward deep, while a counter movement which retreats and rises will lead into backward-high; a movement which retreats and sinks will lead into the direction backward-deep, while a counter movement which advances and rises will lead into forward-high. The peripheral, circular pathway which links these four points of orientation, forward-deep, forward-high, back-ward-high and backward-deep, has been referred to as "the wheel plane."

It follows that three such activities carried out simultaneously will lead into diagonal directions. Thus, to give two examples, a movement, using the right side, which simultaneously rises, opens and advances will lead into the diagonal direction high-right-forward, while a counter movement which sinks, closes and retreats will lead into deep-left-backward. The other six diagonal directions can be arrived at in a similar manner.

Thus, using the right side:
rising, closing and advancing
    will lead into the direction high-left-forward
sinking, opening and retreating
    will lead into the direction deep-right-backward
rising, opening and retreating
    will lead into the direction high-right-backward
sinking, closing and advancing
    will lead into the direction deep-left-forward
rising, closing and retreating
    will lead into the direction high-left-backward
sinking, opening and advancing
    will lead into the direction deep-right-forward

4. AIR PATTERN

We may observe the *air pattern* created by a movement. The pattern traced in the air may be:

FIRST YEAR INFANTS

FOR first year infants dance lessons are a communal activity in which the teacher plays a lively part. Not only will she provide opportunities for the children to respond to as individuals but the teacher will also give encouragement through her personal involvement. "Play" with hands and elbows will often be "showing" teacher and the children derive great pleasure from such unison movements with the teacher as rising, sinking and following and will enjoy approaching and jumping away.

PLATE 1
First year infants involved in movement which shows their need to experience the "total stir" of the body. They are mainly using locomotion but the child at the back is jumping. A number of children are emphasising the use of the knees in the action.

PLATE 2
A general involvement of the whole body in locomotion, with a special concern for hands and arms which are "dancing" high up towards the ceiling.

PLATE 3.—In marked contrast with Plate 2 is this illustration showing a strong element of shared movement. The children are beating their hands rhythmically on the floor, and they are more concerned to enjoy the shared experience with the teacher than to become absorbed individually.

PLATE 4.—Another example of teacher-participation, where the response to the teacher is evident as the children grasp, release and shake their hands.

PLATE 5.—Locomotion with feet widely apart. This naturally forces the child to take long slow steps, with most of the body-weight being taken on the whole of each foot in turn.

PLATE 6.—Locomotion with feet close together. This suggestion produces results which contrast strongly with those shown in Plate 5. Short quick steps are taken and the weight is borne on the toes.

PLATE 7

Another illustration of the total involvement of the whole body in dancing which uses the possibility of being on one or two feet and results in little light hops and jumps.

In Plates 8–9 which follow, the use of a musical instrument is shown for the first time. Such equipment, particularly of the percussive type, is of great value to the teacher as a stimulus and as a rhythmical accompaniment to movement. Later the children themselves may make good use of instruments, and can use them as individual accompaniment—see Plates 22, 23, and 24—or to lead a group—see Plates 44 and 45—or eventually to create an accompaniment for a group rhythm—see Plates 52–58.

PLATE 8

A further illustration showing how, at this age, the children enjoy working in relationship to the teacher. Here we have a concerted rising and sinking movement directly related to a drum rhythm.

PLATE 9

The children can also work in opposition to the teacher. Here they are preparing to rise and she starts to sink.

SECOND YEAR INFANTS.—At this age children retain their pleasure in movement of the whole body but begin to show greater control and awareness of parts of the body involved in the activity.

PLATE 10.—A deliberate attempt has been made to bring the knees into play in deep stepping and in jumps and leaps.

PLATE 11.—The knees are lifted high as a preparation for thrusting the feet firmly into the ground.

PLATE 12.—The task of rising and sinking with firmness and fine touch at choice was given. It is interesting to note the difficulty the children encounter in using the centre of the body. In a number of cases the hips and feet are "rooted" downwards but the child in the centre front manages to rise to her feet and keep a degree of tension through her body. The children are quite able to carry out the movement in their own time; one boy may be seen gripping downward while the majority rise.

PLATES 13 and 13A.—Two photographs showing a rising and sinking sequence with the elbows leading the movement.

PLATES 14–16.—A beginning of dance in twos. In Plate 14 one of each pair dances high while the other accompanies by clapping or beating the floor. In Plate 15 the second partner dances deep and in Plate 16 both dance.

(a) Straight line.
(b) Angular.
(c) Curved.
(d) Twisted.

An angular shape stresses the sharp change of direction and, in execution, brings into play the need to bind and then to free the flow of movement in order to achieve this change. A curved pattern uses a gradual change of direction and is related to a centre which is being surrounded. Clearly, the further the curve progresses the more obvious is this relationship until, with the shaping of a circle, the surrounding of the centre is completed. The expression of a circle is that of wholeness and unity created by the smooth, rounded pathway and by the return to the first point of departure. A spiral pathway keeps this rounded nature but gains an added expression from either the increase or decrease in size or the progression through the space. A twisted pattern involves continual changes of direction as the pathway traced surrounds one centre after another.

5. FLOOR PATTERN

We can observe whether the movement takes place in the space immediately around the body or whether it extends into the general space of the room. We may observe the *floor pattern* which arises. This also may be in the form of a straight, angular, curved or twisted path.

Relationship

I. RELATIONSHIP OF BODY PARTS

We may observe the relationship of *parts of the body* to each other in action or when the movement crystallises into stillness and there is more awareness of body shape.

2. RELATIONSHIP OF INDIVIDUALS

We may observe the relationship of *dancers to each other*. We may observe them near, apart, approaching, parting, surrounding, by the side of, behind, leading, following; moving in unison, in canon, in opposition, in harmony.

3. RELATIONSHIP OF GROUPS

We may observe the relationship of *groups to each other*, as above in 2.

This analysis can be summarised in the following way.

25

SUMMARY OF ANALYSIS.

Aspect 1
THE BODY
WHAT

1. Activity
   (a) Locomotion
   (b) Elevation
   (c) Turns
   (d) Gesture
   (e) Rising, sinking
   (f) Opening, closing
   (g) Advancing, retreating

2. Body part used

3. Symmetry or asymmetry

4. Body Flow—
   simultaneous or
   successive

5. Body shape
   (a) Arrow
   (b) Wall
   (c) Ball
   (d) Screw

Aspect 2
EFFORT
HOW

Motion factors	*Qualities*
1. Weight	Firm
	Fine touch
2. Time	Sudden
	Sustained
3. Space	Direct
	Flexible
4. Flow	Bound
	Free

BASIC EFFORT ACTIONS

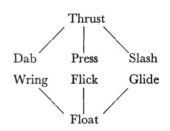

FOUR ASPECTS

Aspect 3 SPACE AND SHAPE WHERE	*Aspect 4* RELATIONSHIP WITH
1. Extension	1. Relatedness of body parts to each other
(a) Small (near) (b) Large (far)	
2. Level	2. Relationship of individuals to each other

(a) High
    (b) Medium
    (c) Deep	

3. Direction	3. Relationship of groups to each other

3. Direction

High	.	.	.	.	Deep
Right	.	.	.	.	Left
Forward		.	.	.	Backward

High-right	.	.	.	Deep-left
Deep-right	.	.	.	High-left
Right-forward		.	.	Left-backward
Right-backward		.	.	Left-forward
Forward-deep		.	.	Backward-high
Backward-deep		.	.	Forward-high

High-right-forward	.	Deep-left-backward
High-left-forward	.	Deep-right-backward
High-left-backward	.	Deep-right-forward
Hight-right-backward	.	Deep-left-forward

4. **Air** Pattern
    (a) Straight line
    (b) Angular shape
    (c) Curved shape
    (d) Twisted shape

5. Floor pattern
    (a) Straight line
    (b) Angular shape
    (c) Curved shape
    (d) Twisted shape

27

This analysis serves in many ways. Firstly, it is a guide to help the teacher to look more closely and specifically at movement, serving as a framework upon which to base observations of movement. Moreover because of its fundamental character it can be used as a basis for looking at any movement—everyday actions, working actions, functional activities and expressive activities.

Such a guide is clearly a valuable aid to any teacher and not only to the movement specialist. The classroom teacher can become aware of the mood of the class, can observe more specifically the body posture and movement characteristics being used and can adapt his attitude accordingly. Thus for example, a teacher arriving to take a class which is talkative and fidgety would do well to participate in this excited mood by darting quick-fire questions which require immediate response. From such a beginning he can put questions which require increasing thought until he establishes a mood of concentration, if he so wishes. The teacher will also be aware of the movement characteristics of each child. So he may appreciate what is at the basis of distinctions between children who may be termed slow and careful, excitable and bubbly, anxious and fussy, controlled and calm, quiet and neat, awkward and clumsy.

Secondly, this analysis serves as the basis from which our material for movement teaching can be selected and so is a help in planning lessons and schemes. Although we make such an analysis for clarification and observation, in fact there is a synthesis of these aspects in bodily action—the body performs rhythmic action in space. Because of this wholeness, many varied starting points can be used. The following examples illustrate this.

A task might derive from Column 1, "The body," and be that of locomotion—stepping. This could be filled out and enriched by the variation of direction and level, by changes of front, by the nearness or distance between the feet, by the speed taken or the resistance used as the steps are made, by the possibilities and pattern which arise when relationship with other dancers is developed.

The task might derive from Column 2, "Effort," and be that of contrast of firmness and fine touch. This could be developed by stressing different parts of the body; for example, the resistance felt in firm pressure of the feet against the floor contrasted with travelling so that the touch of the feet was only gentle; by contrasting the gripping firmness in the hands with their delicate touch; by exploring the possibilities at different levels; by working out an interplay with a partner contrasting firmness with fine touch.

The task might derive from Column 3, "Space," and be that of levels of movement. This could be developed by leading with appropriate body parts, clarifying the air pattern made, varying the dynamics, contrasting leaping and rising and exploring the high level with beating into the floor and sinking down into the deep level.

The task might derive from Column 4, "Relationship," and be that of adaptation to partners. This could be developed by the use of the activities of locomotion, elevation and turns varying the use of bound and free flow, using contrasting effort actions, clarifying the levels and pathways which occur in the meeting, parting, and unison movements of the pair.

In these suggestions the possibilities of development have certainly not been exhausted.

A third use of this analysis of movement is that it provides a good framework for the teacher to have in mind when helping the child to develop his own understanding and observation of movement. As one child watches another, he can become increasingly aware of the possibilities and general principles underlying quite diverse individual movement phrases and sequences, and later dances. This may involve, for example, noting whether the jumps are off or on to one or two feet, noting the accent in a phrase, observing the levels through which the movement passes. These are all definite points for a child to observe and such specific observations have more urpose than his being asked to watch another child with no pointers to guide him in what to look for.

Further familiarity with the analysis enables the teacher to aid the children to develop and clarify their own movement sequences. This could take the form of drawing attention to the function of a less active part of the body, suggesting that the sequence needs clarifying from the point of view of stress or timing, or clarification of the levels and directions used.

So this analysis forms the basis upon which the movement vocabulary can be built. That various aspects are more suitable as starting points for different age groups is of course true. This has been indicated by Laban in

29

Modern Educational Dance in the chapters "Dancing through the Age Groups" and "Sixteen Basic Movement-Themes."

The link between the eight themes suggested as appropriate for children of infant and junior age and the analysis of the four aspects already tabulated is summarised as follows:

Theme 1. Themes concerned with the awareness of the body—*body aspect.*

Theme 2. Themes concerned with the awareness of force and time—*effort aspect.*

Theme 3. Themes concerned with the awareness of space—*space aspect.*

Theme 4. Themes concerned with the awareness of the flow of the weight of the body in space and time—*effort aspect.*

Theme 5. Themes concerned with the adaptation to partners—*relationship aspect.*

Theme 6. Themes concerned with the instrumental use of the limbs of the body—*body aspect.*

Theme 7. Themes concerned with the awareness of isolated actions—*effort aspect.*

Theme 8. Themes concerned with occupational rhythms—*effort* and *body aspects.*

CHAPTER 3

The structure of the syllabus

"THE leading idea is that the teacher should find his own manner of stimulating the pupils to move, and later to dance, by choosing from a collection of basic movement-themes those variations which are appropriate to the actual stage and state of development of the pupil or of the majority of the class. . . The movement ideas contained in one theme need not be fully assimilated by a pupil before another theme is started" (Laban).

Clearly Laban, in laying great stress on the need for the teacher to observe and select appropriate themes for the children, intended the basic movement-themes to be a guide. In planning an actual syllabus for infant and junior children these themes can be used together with the detailed analysis set out in the previous chapter. The teacher's approach to the work must also take into consideration two clear stages in the learning process.

Infants and Juniors: A suggested syllabus

Stage 1. First the young infant is at the stage where he learns directly from personal experience and action. His knowledge of himself must derive from personal experience and experiment in movement. Thus he will whirl around until he collapses on the ground, hop on one foot attempting to keep his balance, roll across the floor until he meets a piece of furniture which arrests the flow of movement, or bounce up and down on any springy surface. He will manipulate anything within his grasp and so learn, for example, something of the tension needed to screw or unscrew or something of the problems encountered in releasing a building block from the hand so that it remains balanced on top of others. He needs to experience what might be called the "total stir" of the body (see Plate 1). He needs to enjoy the fun of movement. From such bodily actions the infant, as the primitive man before him, finds himself at one with his world. At this stage then we shall expect the child to produce an immediate response to the stimulus of words, to the tone of voice, to a variety of sounds. We shall expect him to enjoy the explorations and discoveries of what he can do with his body, to enjoy the feeling of repetition when doing an activity over and over again and to enjoy the fun of the unexpected movement happening.

It follows that the concern of the teacher must be to provide him with opportunities to discover his own capacities, to stimulate the child into absorbing activities, to provide further experiences and to encourage experiment.

Stage 2. This stage will grow out of the first and will be developed through the top infant and junior school. In this second stage the child begins to be able to use his activities to get data about the world into his mind and there transform them so that they can be used selectively to solve problems. He can however still only "structure" immediately present reality and has not reached the stage of conjuring up systematically the full range of alternative possibilities that could exist. It is therefore still important for him to be presented with learning situations which are immediate and real and in which pertinent questions will lead him to *understand* something of the world of movement as well as *experience* it, as will the young infant. To quote Laban again:

> "Each of the basic movement-themes represents a movement idea corresponding to a stage in the progressive *unfolding of the feel of movement in the growing child,* and in later stages to the *development of his mental understanding of the principles involved*" (my italics).

At this second stage then we shall find the children able to build sequences and dances which are their own invention, and in which there is relationship between "what" moves, "how" it moves, "where" it moves. Moreover they will have become more able to work with others and to establish relationships in groups.

A more detailed scheme of work for the primary school follows. It is set out year by year using the four aspects already covered in the previous chapters and making cross-references to the themes Laban has suggested should be mainly used at the appropriate stages. In the suggested scheme of material for the infant school, the work has been set out in two broad age groups only. This is because of the wide age ranges found in infant classes in practice and because of the growing use of family grouping.

Stage 1: Infants

Infants, first year: material to be covered

BODY AWARENESS—LABAN THEME I

Activities which involve the "total stir of the whole being" are most appropriate (see also Plates 1–9). These include stepping and running, galloping and skipping, spinning and turning, leaping, hopping and jumping and locomotion on all fours. Experience shows that children at this stage of their development find it difficult to stop the flow of movement.

Body parts: in addition to the activities involving the whole body, exploration of possibilities with the extremities can take place. *Feet* will be used in beating on the floor, in travelling on the heels and on the toes, in coming close to each other, in taking big wide steps and in kicking. *Hands* will be used for grasping and releasing, shaking, beating the floor, clapping and tapping. *Knees* will be much in evidence in hopping and jumping.

EFFORT—LABAN THEME 2

Speed can be experienced in variations of quick and slow, especially with the help of sound.

Weight can be experienced in the strength of gripping hands and pushing the feet into the floor. In "pushing" feet the result is not a sustained pressure but this word-suggestion seems to produce more strength than the word "stamping." Contrasts can be achieved through loud and soft stepping and hand-beating, through vigorous leaping and jumping and quiet light-footed stepping and creeping.

SPACE—LABAN THEME 3

Near and far can be explored as contrasted experiences in stepping with the feet and in body shape. Exploration can be made of areas above, near and on the ground, in front, behind, sideways (but not left and right). Left to dance freely, children show a marked preference for travelling forwards and for spinning and turning, covering the ground and on the

C   33

spot. This will be done with varied methods of locomotion and elevation and even combinations of activities, such as jumping and turning on the spot at the same time.

RELATIONSHIP—LABAN THEME 5

At this age the child works as an individual within the mood of the whole group and in relationship with the teacher. Children will make unison movements within the teacher, e.g. dancing high and dancing deep or rising and sinking or following. They also enjoy such activities as dancing after teacher and stopping as she turns, approaching her and darting away from her.

Infants, second year: additional material

BODY AWARENESS—LABAN THEME 1

The activities of rising and sinking, spreading and shrinking, involving the capacity to move between extremes, can be introduced (see also Plates 10-16). The mixing of activities to make short phrases involving spinning, travelling and leaping will be possible. These may be in sequence, e.g. travelling followed by jumping or they may be combined, e.g. jumping while turning.

Body parts: knees will be brought into play in deep stepping which emphasises the use of knees, and in jumps and leaps with knees shooting high. *Elbows* will be involved in meeting and parting, in pointing sharply into space and in "dancing" on the floor and in the air.

EFFORT—LABAN THEME 2

Speed will be experienced through gradual changes. While a slow increase of speed is possible for children of this age, gradual decrease remains difficult.

Time: The qualities will mainly be experienced as contrasts of quick and slow, but sometimes the children achieve real suddenness and sustainment in meeting and parting of body parts.

Weight: The qualities of weight can be experienced in the thrusting and pressing of the feet into the floor, the pushing up from the floor with the

34

whole body and the gripping of body parts towards the centre of the body. Lightness will be felt in the release after gripping, in stepping and in play with the hands. The children can respond to broad rhythmic phrases e.g. a slow firm beat on a drum followed by a shaking phrase on a tambourine.

SPACE—LABAN THEMES 3 AND 4

The children can use straight, curved, roundabout and twisted pathways. They can move forwards, backwards and sideways using body parts to lead the movement. They can use high, medium, deep levels and link near and far in various directions around the body.

RELATIONSHIP—LABAN THEME 5

At this stage there is an increased awareness of the general space and positive use is made of it but there remains a tendency to avoid others rather than to work with them. Nevertheless a beginning can be made of work in twos such as simple sequences where children dance alternately or both together, although they cannot yet achieve real sensitivity in co-operation. Continued enjoyment of the dance relationship with the teacher will be experienced.

In general a greater independence is developed by the children in building their own rhythms, phrases and sequences.

Stage 2: Juniors

As has already been stated in the introduction to this syllabus, Stage 2 will grow out of Stage 1. There will be considerable overlap of material used at the top of the infant school and the bottom of the junior school. It must be stressed that the age ranges given are merely a general guide. It is the gradual transition and spiral progression of the work which is important.

Juniors, first year, aged 7–8: material to be covered

In addition to that already outlined for infants, progress will be made in the following aspects.

BODY AWARENESS—LABAN THEME I

Body parts can be used in leading a movement outwards from the centre, inwards to the centre and around the body. The children can use knees leading to a step and elbows leading in air patterns. (See Plates 17–24.)

EFFORT—LABAN THEMES 2, 3 AND 4

Increased ability is evident in the children's use of the qualities of weight and time.

Weight—firmness and fine touch: experience of firmness is gained in stepping, jumping, "making a strong statue," gripping in towards the centre of body, pressing up away from the floor, pressing down into the floor. Experience of fine touch is gained in stepping, in light jumps, in relaxing and opening from gripped positions. Grip and release can be combined in a phrase.

Time—suddenness and sustainment: experience of suddenness can be gained in quick darting movements, sudden turns and jumps, quick gestures of hands. Experience of sustainment can be gained in the separating and meeting of the hands, in rising and sinking, in spreading and closing. Problems of balance make stepping with sustainment difficult.

Flow—free and bound: contrasts can be experienced between continuity in leaping and travelling, rolling and turning on the one hand and in arresting the flow of movement in stopping on the other.

SPACE—LABAN THEME 3

Experiences will include the use of straight, wavy, curved and twisted pathways on the floor and air patterns which curve and twist. Difficulty will still be encountered with the sharp angles of zigzag pathways.

RELATIONSHIP—LABAN THEME 5

Adaptation to partners will be experienced in action, reaction, response sequences and the use of contrasting qualities and levels. Groups of three can work together, meeting, parting, mingling, moving in unison and developing sequences. Larger groups will have the ability to follow the leader's activities, pathways, levels, speeds.

In general it is at this stage that the child becomes aware of the synthesis of the various aspects of movement. Thus he can work with others and he is able to use the distinctive qualities and, at one and the same time, spatial organisation, provided that sequences are short. At this age they can dance with instruments provided that they can be held in one hand and provided that they do not demand the mastery of the control which is necessary to make contact between beater and drum. The sound in fact results directly from the movement.

Juniors, second year, aged 8–9: material developing from the previous work

BODY AWARENESS—LABAN THEMES I AND 6

Activities: increased ability will enable the children to distinguish between the five basic jumps in using elevation.

Arm and leg gestures will be used in gathering, scattering and penetrating the space. Awareness of the shape of the body in space, in stillness and in motion is very evident. (See Plates 25–30.)

EFFORT—LABAN THEME 2

Combinations of the qualities of weight and time can now be made giving (a) firmness with suddenness, (b) fine touch with suddenness, (c) firmness with sustainment, (d) fine touch with sustainment.

Firm and sudden qualities can be combined in the sudden gripping of the whole body, in energetic leaps which burst upwards into the air, in downward jumps stressing the accent into the floor, in explosive turning jumps, in the sharp shooting out of elbows, knees and feet and in rhythmical beating and travelling with the feet. The beating of a drum or tambourine can be a helpful accompaniment.

Fine touch and sudden qualities can be combined in excited darting, flickering, quivering hand gestures, in the light shooting out and back of the feet, in the tapping of the floor with the feet, in hasty jumps, turns and travelling which give an experience of surprise or shock. Marraccas, skulls, castanets and bells can be helpful for accompaniment.

Firm and sustained qualities can be combined in slow contraction of the whole body, in the tension of pulling parts of the body away from each other, in the pressing together of body parts, in screwing down towards the ground, in turning and twisting using backs, shoulders and elbows, in pressing out into the space using hands and other body parts to lead. It is difficult to get sustained strength with percussion sound but a continuous strong drum beat can sometimes be helpful.

Fine touch and sustained qualities can be combined in gentle spreading and turning of the whole body, in "airborne" rising, in smoothing, waving, undulating gestures of the hands and as a transition to relaxation after firm, sustained action as above. The soft playing of a large cymbal or gong, a shaken tambourine, a xylophone, or smoothing the parchment of a drum can be helpful as accompaniment.

SPACE—LABAN THEME 3

In addition to the use of pathways, levels and varied extensions, the main area of progress is in relation to body awareness, with the development of the feeling for body shape and the relatedness of parts of the body to each other.

RELATIONSHIP—LABAN THEME 5

The children will enjoy working in groups to create dance sequences which show contrasts, the development of phrases, the use of climax and co-operation with others.

In general it is at this age that they can most effectively handle instruments and dance with them.

Juniors, third year, aged 9–10: material developing from the previous work

BODY AWARENESS—LABAN THEME I

This will be evident in more awareness of symmetry and asymmetry, and of simultaneous and successive body flow. (See Plates 31–45.)

EFFORT—LABAN THEMES 3, 4 AND 7

Space—directness and flexibility: experience of directness is gained in travelling over the floor in straight pathways, in gestures cutting through

the space. Experience of flexibility is gained in turning and twisting, in weaving in roundabout pathways through the space, in arm
gestures involving the use of the space all around the body. Combinations of these qualities with those of weight and time can be
experienced.

Direct and firm qualities can be combined in forceful, boring, cleaving,
penetrating gestures through the space using finger-tips, fists, elbows, flats
of feet and in downward driving with feet stressing powerful, purposeful
action.

Direct and fine touch qualities can be combined in gentle smoothing
gestures which glide rather than bore through the space and in skimming
across the floor from place to place.

Direct and sudden qualities can be combined in shooting upwards from a
crouched position on the floor, in gestures using fingers, elbows and feet
to pierce the space with definite focus and aim, in jumps straight up into
the air and pouncing down on to a spot on the floor.

Direct and sustained qualities can be combined in slow upward rising with
emphasis on the gradual threading of the body straight through the space.
It can be experienced in slow, clear-cut gestures using the finger tips or edge
of the hand and in unhurried, purposeful stepping in an undeviating pathway.

Flexible and firm qualities can be combined in screwing, twisting arm and
leg gestures which use counter-tension and in the turning, twisting and
knotting of the whole body. Emphasis must be placed in all flexible actions
on the mobility of the joints and the extension of parts of the body into
different areas of the space.

Flexible and fine touch qualities can be combined in gentle weightless stirring,
twirling and travelling using rising, spreading and turning and in delicate,
undulating inter-weaving of hands and arms.

Flexible and sudden qualities can be combined in hasty changes of position
of hands, in sharp changes of direction, in sudden, lively, "surprise" jumps
and turns.

Flexible and sustained qualities can be combined in slow weaving in and out
of each other using rising and sinking, twisting and turning in a roundabout, slow-motion manner.

39

SPACE—LABAN THEME 3

There will be further progress made in the clarification of the shape of the body, both in movement and in stillness, alone and with others and also in the area of space used. The many directions, pathways and levels can be used confidently and, as has been indicated under the heading "Effort" above, it is at this age that the child is capable of showing clear differentiation between direct and flexible action in space.

RELATIONSHIP—LABAN THEME 5

At this stage the children show increasing sensitivity when working together. This enables progress to be made in group sequences and dances which involve awareness of group shape and stress the relationship of one child to another to create a whole. The development of group motifs can also take place. The test to apply here is that the motif created is dependent upon the interplay of everyone in the group and could not be achieved by an individual. In general more use can be made of music, although the children can perfectly well make their own rhythms and do not need to rely on music.

Juniors, fourth year, aged 10–11: material developing from the previous work

BODY AWARENESS—LABAN THEME 1

There will be increased awareness of relatedness of parts of the body to each other. (See Plates 46–60.)

EFFORT—LABAN THEMES 7 AND 8

Basic effort actions: combinations will be made of the qualities of weight, time and space. Repetition of these effort actions will bring out their rhythmic nature. Effort transitions will occur in working actions. Experience can be given of different time rhythms and the placing of accent in a phrase.

Thrust: this will be most easily experienced in stepping, jumping, galloping with the accent into the ground and in the use of driving gestures with such parts of the body as fists, elbows, feet, knees. The contrast can

First Year Juniors
At this age the children have an increased awareness of the use of different parts of the body. They can differentiate between the weight and time qualities and are beginning to work more co-operatively with others to build simple dance phrases and sequences.

Plates 17 and 18
These illustrations show that at this stage the children have the ability to make sudden jumps and turns in the air and can bind the flow of the movement to hold their endings. The two photographs show clearly how young children follow a natural tendency to associate vigorous movement such as leaps and turns with extension, and stillness with contraction. A higher degree of mastery is necessary to enable the child to arrive at and maintain stillness in an extended bodily shape. See Plates 48 and 49.

PLATES 19 and 20

The task set was for the children to meet and mingle in small groups. The boys responded with movements which used different levels and unusual "play" with fingers, wrists and elbows, while in Plate 20 the use of backs, hips and knees is evident.

These movements, which were performed to a drum accompaniment, had a staccato rhythmical quality and proved a source of fun for the boys.

PLATE 21
These girls were set the same task of meeting and mingling in small groups. They responded with a fine touch, careful movement and with a sensitivity to each other.

PLATE 22
At this age children can use instruments provided that these can be held in the hand so that the sound results from the movement. This boy has developed a repetitive phrase of travelling and jumping.

PLATE 23
This boy is engaged in a less dynamic action than the previous one but clearly obtains great enjoyment from making his own sound.
He uses small steps with a clear rhythmical beating of the tambourine which, held high, brings about the upright body shape in contrast to the "ball-like" shape of the boy in Plate 22.

PLATE 24
Of interest in this photograph is the fact that while some children are content to dance alone, others form groups from their choice. These three boys have achieved quite a degree of co-operation, probably helped by the fact that two are twin brothers.

Second Year Juniors

At this stage the children show increased co-ordination and mastery of movement. They become aware of the relatedness of body parts; they can combine the weight and time qualities to give rhythmicality to the movement and their interpretation of a task or suggestion shows more individuality.

Plate 25

Here the movement experience was that of parting the hands with sustainment and bringing them together with suddenness to create a simple rhythmical phrase.

28

PLATE 26

PLATE 26
Movement involving free travelling and leap-ing shows an increasing awareness of the relatedness of parts of the body to each other and thus greater clarity in the shape of the body in action. This is particularly evident in the use of arms and hands.

PLATE 27
The response of the children to the task of energetic upward leaps and strong downward steps and jumps

PLATE 28
The task set was to dance away from the floor and into the floor with clear use of the body parts active or leading the movement. Thus we can observe the energetic leap bursting into the air of the child to the right and the one in the centre foreground, while another child at the back is rising high with her elbow leading. In both 27 and 28 we see greater co-ordination and mastery and more individual interpreta-tion of the task.

At this age it is evident that whilst the children still enjoy spontaneous energetic movement they are gaining an awareness of the shape of the body in space. They can now consciousiy discipline their ideas. Thus in Plates 27 and 28 the particular intention of each child is clearly indicated, and the movement imagination is revealed in the rich variety of action used. These opportunities to shape their own activ-ities serve to build up confidence.

PLATES 29 and 30.—These two photographs were taken during a pair sequence. The framework given was that one child (A) should dance high and with fine touch to meet (B) who danced deeply with firmness. The sequence was to be completed by either changing levels with or without turning and twisting, or jumping away to their original place. If the comparison is made with 14, 15 and 16, it will be seen that the children of Junior age have a greater capacity to react to each other, as well as added bodily mastery.

be experienced between the final impact of a thrust performed with bound flow and the energy which streams onwards in a free flow thrust.

Dab: this will be most easily experienced by the use of the extremities, in light running, pin-pointing on the floor, tapping with the feet, in sharp upward movement of the knees, in quick darting out and back with the fingers. This is usually free flow but can be bound.

Press: this will most easily be experienced in the pressure of one hand against another, in pressure of feet against the floor, in the pressing together and pulling apart of body parts to stress the counter-tension. Pressing is a controlled movement performed with bound flow.

Slash: this will most easily be experienced in the whipping action of arms and legs, the action being of a scattering successive free flow nature. It is helpful to use turning jumps with an asymmetric stress.

Float: this will be most easily experienced in buoyant, weightless stirring and turning, rising and spreading, twisting and weaving in and out of each other with roundabout pathways and plasticity of the body through the use of many directions for the joints and body parts. The contrast can be experienced between the more guided movement as performed with bound flow and the greater fluency in free flow.

Wring: this will be most easily experienced in strong turning and twisting with tension in the body and the use of downward directions, bound flow and counter-tension, although the flow can be free.

Flick: this will be most easily experienced in fingers and wrists moving in a quick, lively, roundabout way, in light turns and leaps and scattering gestures, using free flow.

Glide: this will be most easily experienced in smoothing gestures using palms and marking clear straight bound flow pathways through the space, in rising upwards and in stepping, although this is more difficult because of balance.

SPACE—LABAN THEMES 3 AND 5

The space around his own body and the general space of the room will be used in a discriminating manner by the child of this age who has had some experience in dance. He will be able to lead a group with such actions as leaping, galloping and fast travelling, avoiding other groups and creating interesting pathways. In a group dance the sense of pattern which will develop from the relationships takes on more significance and these patterns will become clarified with further practice and repetition.

RELATIONSHIP—LABAN THEME 5

The children will be able to work in groups of six and seven with active co-operation. Interaction of groups upon each other can take place. This interaction of groups will lead to the development of dances involving the whole class. In general, at this stage, a wide variety of instruments can be handled to help to establish rhythms and to bring out different movement qualities or effort actions.

The dances will show the ability to integrate the various aspects of movement—body awareness, appropriate effort quality, clarity of shape and full use of the space, a real sense of relationship.

Movement memory will have improved and the children will want to repeat sequences and dances they have created. Experience has shown that children will become intensely enthusiastic about a dance of their own creation. They will think about it between lessons, will make all manner of suggestions to improve or develop it and will show great pleasure in re-creating it. So true is this that they will want to dance it for others to see, not as a performance but as a piece of communal creative work.

CHAPTER 4

The structure of the lesson

"Children should invent their dances freely as a creative activity very similar to that fostered in modern art education." *Laban**

THE actual planning of lessons will vary with the gifts, training and experience of the teacher but, for students and young teachers in particular, *one* suggestion for planning a lesson is described here since it has proved helpful for beginners.

It will be recalled that four aspects of the observation of movement can be distinguished, aspects which we have called observation of the body itself, of the effort, of space and shape, and observation of relationship.† In planning an actual lesson, the fourth of these—relationship—being fundamental to all dance must always be included. One of the other three—the body, effort, space—should then be chosen to provide the *main theme* of the lesson which, whenever possible, should use the duality of the aspect selected. Thus, for example, suitable main themes might be movement contrasted with stillness, firmness contrasted with fine touch, angular air pattern contrasted with curved air pattern, dancing alone contrasted with dancing with a partner.

In addition, a *subsidiary theme* should be chosen from one of the two remaining aspects—the body, effort, space.

Planned in this way the lesson should have considerable variety and richness of movement ideas and, most important, that sense of the unity of bodily action from which these aspects derive will be preserved.

A suggested plan

In order to clarify the structure of this one type of lesson, further details of the possible development of material are suggested below.

* *Modern Educational Dance.*   † See Analysis, Chapter 2.

Infants (Reception Class)

If the main theme selected to be taken was BODY AWARENESS—in particular feet and hands, then suitable subsidiary themes could be EFFORT—lively and vigorous contrasted with gentle and quiet, and RELATIONSHIP—dancing with the teacher contrasted with dancing alone.

Among the experiences which could be included in such a lesson are:

Feet dancing strongly: leaping, jumping, beating, travelling freely about the space to a vigorous drum or tambourine accompaniment. The phrase could be varied in length with the use of definite stops. Repetition of the same phrase a number of times would give a rhythm.

Feet dancing lightly on the spot and round and round with small near steps.

Feet dancing all over the space with light, soft, gentle steps, hardly touching the floor, unaccompanied or with gentle playing of bells or xylophone.

Contrast of the two ways of dancing—vigorous and lively with quiet and gentle.

Hands lightly dancing away from each other about the space contrasted with firm strong gripping together and even clapping.

Hands tapping the floor gently contrasted with firm and loud beating.

Hands beating and tapping the floor contrasted with dancing high towards the ceiling and round and round with the feet also active.

This could be developed into a final sequence such as: The class start around and near to the teacher, hands touching the floor. Keeping level with the teacher, hands rise upwards with excited quivering movements. They dance near the ceiling and round and round. The feet join in and this leads to vigorous lively dancing individually about the space. As the instrument becomes quiet, or at another sound, the children gradually gather around teacher again and sink down ready to begin the sequence again.

Top Infants

If the main theme to be developed was to deal with the sudden and sustained aspects of EFFORT, then suitable subsidiary themes could be SPACE AWARENESS—high and deep levels, closed and open body shapes; and RELATIONSHIPS—pairs.

Such experiences could be included as: quick, lively, sudden darting and stepping all over the room. This could be taken freely and as a response to the playing of a castanet or shaken tambourine or little bells, using a repeated rhythmic phrase.

On the spot, sudden downward inward gripping and closing could contrast with sustained spreading and rising. Attention should be drawn to grip in the hands, elbows, chest and back, legs and to release in the whole body. This could be taken with rhythmic repetition and gradual extension in the opening and rising.

Sudden jumps, turns, excited travelling to a new place could end with a clear stop followed by slower travelling back to the teacher. This should be repeated a number of times.

Working near to the teacher to echo her changes between the situations of deep, high, closed and spreading wide could follow.

This could be developed into a final sequence such as: working with a partner, starting apart, proceeds to quick, lively, darting travel to meet the partner and finish still in clear body shape, e.g. stretched high, near the floor, closed up or spread out. One of the pair makes a sustained change of situation—rising or sinking or closing or opening. The other follows and echoes this. After several changes and echoes, they can burst away suddenly or dance off alone again.

Juniors 8–9 years

If the main theme to be developed was BODY SHAPE—ball, arrow, screw, then suitable subsidiary themes could be EFFORT—sudden and sustained, bound and free flow and RELATIONSHIP—small groups.

Such experiences could be included as:

Free dancing. At the drum beat stop firmly, holding a clear body shape.

Starting with a closed "ball-like" body shape, opening to a wide shape. This could be done with firmness, with suddenness, with sustainment. The child should be asked to make clear which part of the body is active or leading, whether it is a more successive or simultaneous body flow and whether the final attitude is symmetric or asymmetric.

From a closed starting position, spreading with firmness and sustainment

45

followed by sudden contracting, closing, with spiralling and travelling to a new place. Repetition of this would give a rhythmic phrase.

From a "ball-like" starting position, shooting out into an "arrow" shape, stressing the linear shape and the penetration towards one definite spot in the space. Extension of the size of the movement could lead to leaping and rushing through the space. Binding and arresting the flow of the movement will crystallise into an arrow-like shape.

Travelling with twisting and turning, in and out of each other, high and deep and stopping the flow of movement in what should be a twisted body shape. This can be done with varying degrees of firmness, with freely flowing movement and more controlled bound flow. Use of hips, shoulders, elbows, backs must be encouraged.

An individual sequence can be created using twisting and turning and screwing into a tight shape and shooting out into an arrow-like shape.

This could be developed into a final sequence such as: working in small groups, starting a little away, twisting, turning and weaving in and out, high and deep to arrive in a final twisted group shape; shooting out into more linear "arrow-like" shape and then drawing back together with firm sustainment. This could be repeated several times to create a rhythm. It could be left to the group to decide the number of times of the shooting away and drawing together; to decide whether the shooting was individually away from the others or whether it was a group movement; to clarify the directions selected and to bring the sequence to a finish as they wished.

Juniors 10–11 years

If the main theme to be developed was EFFORT—the basic effort actions of thrust, press, float and flick, then suitable subsidiary themes could be BODY—the use of appropriate activities, and RELATIONSHIP—group rhythms.

Such experience could be included as:

Individual experience of the single efforts and of pairs that are akin.

Thrusting (firm, sudden and direct) could be experienced through the feet thrusting into the ground, the knees into the air, the whole body leaping upward, the fists and elbows punching out into the space and returning to the centre of the body.

Pressing (firm, sustained and direct) could be experienced through the slowing down of the thrusting, pulling apart body parts such as the hands and elbows, pushing parts together, pressing the whole body down into the ground, pushing up away from the ground, using backs, shoulders, elbows. Thrusting and pressing could be linked by several repeated sudden rhythmic discharges of energy being followed by sustained pressure.

Floating (fine touch, sustained and flexible). The opposite effort to thrusting could be experienced through buoyant and light rising, weightless travelling and turning.

Flicking (fine touch, sudden and flexible) could be experienced through a hurrying of the floating to achieve sudden excited bursts of movement, with turns and jumps, keeping the fine touch.

Floating and flicking could be linked by a buoyant, unhurried, weightless stirring becoming excited with sudden flicking of hands and feet.

This could be developed into a final sequence working together in groups of about seven. A choice could be given of either thrusting and pressing or floating and flicking. A group motif could be developed by the children, clarifying the length of each part of the rhythmic phrase, either working towards each other or towards a common direction, using the same or different body parts, varying levels, dancing on the spot or travelling. The sequence could further be developed if one of the two efforts used became predominant. Possibilities of interaction with other groups could also be developed in another lesson.

It must be made very clear that this suggested plan is of *one possible structure of lesson* and *not* the structure of every lesson. The gifted or experienced teacher will be able to sense the needs of the children, select appropriate material instinctively and plan his own lessons as he thinks fit. Clearly teaching is as creative an activity as dancing. The lesson material too may derive much more naturally from the particular interest of the class in some topic or in some special school activity or seasonal enthusiasm. It may derive from a starting point other than movement itself. However, the lesson is primarily concerned with what Laban called "effort exercise" and it is abundantly evident that, although there is much interest in teaching dance, considerable help is needed to give security to those beginning such work.

47

It is sometimes suggested that modern educational dance can only be taught by the most able, but as in other subjects it must be just as possible for the average teacher to be successful. The primary teacher in particular has the exciting task of educating the whole child and he develops fundamental attitudes and approaches which permeate the teaching of many subjects. His method of approach will frequently be to present a theme or topic, to stimulate the children's interest in the idea presented and then encourage them to set to work to explore the material and, from their explorations, create something of their own, either individually or with others. This is similar to the procedure already suggested in the examples of dance lessons given. There the theme is introduced, the children are guided to experience the possibilities inherent in it and are then given scope to play with the movement idea and, where this is appropriate, to invent and to clarify.

All this takes time—time for the young ones to explore and to repeat and to get caught up in the flow of movement. It takes even more time for the older ones who have reached the next stage—time to explore, to experiment, to select, to reject, to invent and create, to discipline the first efforts, to develop movement memory. In this way mastery of movement is gained. Dances of increasing length and complexity can only be created as this mastery grows. This is also true of the child's efforts in language and indeed in all the arts.

Asking the Right Questions

Even in the shortest sequence, the first improvisations must be clarified and the child challenged to show clearly in his body the answers to many questions. With young children questions can be used to stimulate their movement imagination. On the other hand for the older ones in Stage 2 the questions will help them select and clarify and build sequences which can be remembered and form the basis for dance composition.

The kind of questions to be asked are:

Of the body

Activities and flow: "What are you doing—stepping, running, leaping, spinning, turning, holding still?"

48

31

THIRD YEAR JUNIORS

AT this stage the children have more concern for the shape of the body in movement and in stillness. They can use contrasts of symmetric and asymmetric body shape and will be able to use both successive and simultaneous body flow in the process of moving from one situation to another.

The use of spatial qualities enhances their use of weight and time and their ability to relate to each other in creative work shows a marked development.

PLATE 31

The arrival at the end of a phrase of movement.

PLATE 32

An awareness of the shape of the body is shown by this boy whose movement brought in some twist of the body while retaining a symmetric use of the arms. In comparing this with the girl in Plate 25 there is a clear contrast in body shape and in the expression of the movement, which is more active on the part of the boy and calmer on the part of the girl.

32

PLATE 33
Forceful penetration of the space is being carried out with fists and elbows directing the movement.

PLATE 34
These boys are combining firmness and flexibility in twisted roundabout pathways.

Although the floor pattern is free, there is an obvious sensitivity of the children to each other, which appears in the relatedness of body parts.

PLATES 35 and 36
In these two photographs the qualities of fine touch and flexibility are combined. The gentle, weightless stirring, turning and rising with a delicate use of the hands can be contrasted with the grip and tension shown in Plates 33 and 34.

PLATE 37

In this photograph the qualities of fine touch and flexibility are combined but, in contrast to the slow stirring action in Plates 35 and 36, children here use sudden lively jumps and "surprise" arrivals. The girl on the left is caught at a moment of suspension. All show an awareness of body shape in action.

In these photographs we see the growing ability of children of this age to relate to each other in groups. This may be in a spontaneous free way, as in Plates 33–37, or can be more organised as in Plates 38, 39, and the sequence shown in Plates 40–43. The form and structure of a dance sequence should emerge gradually as a result of repetition and consequent clarification, rather than as a result of deliberate organisation.

PLATES 38 and 39

These three boys have created a brief dance in which they meet with sustainment and part with suddenness. They have a concentrated, bound flow attitude in the meeting in which they are aware of a relatedness to the centre space which is formed between them. In the parting they use jumping turns to emphasise the speed of parting.

37

PLATES 40–43
The framework for the task set in this
group of photographs was to meet,
for one to lead the others, and to con-
clude in whatever way seemed appropriate. The pattern and some aspect
of the relationship was therefore set.
The bodily activities, the body parts
to be used, the qualities selected and
the resolution of the situation was left
to the children. Plate 40 shows the
approach, with the girl on the right
advancing firmly with elbow leading
while the one on the left almost wards
off the approach. In Plate 41 the left-
hand girl has confronted the other.
The drawing along of the three by
the one is shown in Plate 42, while
Plate 43 shows the final movement
when the three have broken away
and the leader herself turns away.

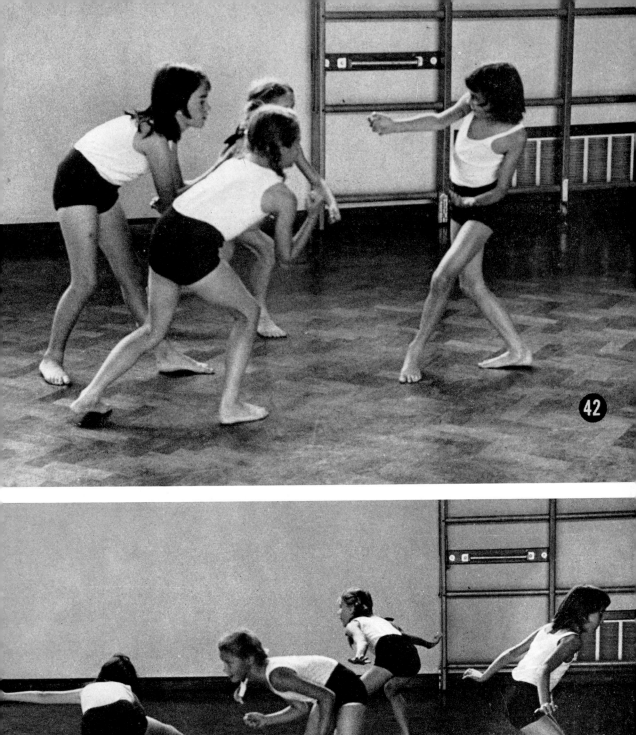

42

43

PLATES 44 and 45.—Free work, in groups. The leader in Plate 44 is playing a rhythm to which the group responds. The boys had a percussive stepping with the last one driving the line along, so that an air of comedy was created.

The mixed group in Plate 45 danced around a centre following the leader with travelling and leaping.

FOURTH YEAR JUNIORS

FOURTH year juniors have the capacity to integrate the various aspects of movement—body awareness, dynamic context and clarity of form. Their dance compositions reveal not only this mastery but also sensitivity to each other and the enjoyment of a shared creation.

PLATE 46

This class was able to achieve the basic effort action of floating and found the word "weightless" a great help in experiencing buoyancy.

PLATE 47

The effort action of thrusting used in a meeting of a group of girls. They have the ability to show a clear use of the body, with a definite action, a clarity of shape and a real relationship to each other.

Although the general focus is downward, the girls give the group shape a clear depth through the arm gestures.

PLATES 48 and 49
Here the effort action of pressing is used as the boys approach each other. As with the girls, they have the capacity to work sensitively together. In this class, the boys tend to prefer to come very close to each other. This they can achieve without losing concentration.

PLATE 50

This group of girls makes an interesting group shape with their pressing action. They started at different levels and selected the body part to lead the movement and to relate them to each other. These pressing actions were linked by a lighter transition, thus giving a rhythm.

PLATE 51

A further illustration of the point made earlier: that these boys enjoy forming compact groups. They also like the unusual possibilities inherent in the movement situation.

While in Plate 48 the intention is to surround the centre space formed between them, in this illustration the boys fill the space and a situation of a more dramatic nature is created.

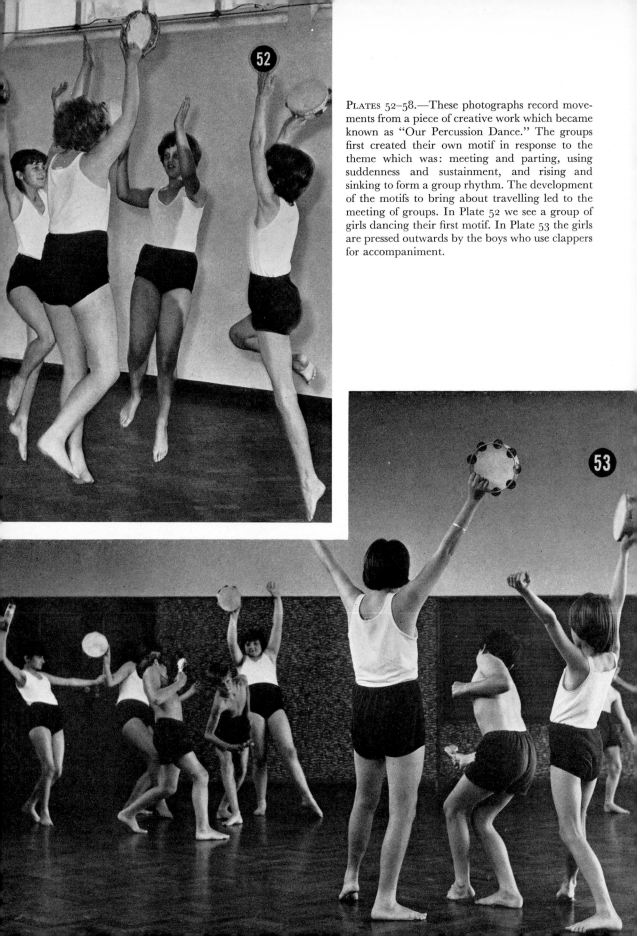

PLATES 52–58.—These photographs record movements from a piece of creative work which became known as "Our Percussion Dance." The groups first created their own motif in response to the theme which was: meeting and parting, using suddenness and sustainment, and rising and sinking to form a group rhythm. The development of the motifs to bring about travelling led to the meeting of groups. In Plate 52 we see a group of girls dancing their first motif. In Plate 53 the girls are pressed outwards by the boys who use clappers for accompaniment.

In Plate 54 the previous relationship is reversed as the girls drive the boys in to the centre. In Plate 55 we see a group of boys completing their first motif. In Plates 56 and 57 the girls surround the boys and enclose them with firm stepping and a final rising over them. This group of girls chose to use voice sounds as accompaniment.

In Plates 56 and 57 the girls surround the boys with a firm stepping action in which they take up the **boys'** drum beat. Finally, in Plate 58, the girls rise over the boys using a repetitive closing, rising action **and** reverting to their earlier accompaniment of voice sound.

The group dance illustrated in Plates 52–58 shows how well boys and girls can work together in creative dance. To be able to achieve this they involve the effort qualities, the spatial concepts and the movement ideas previously experienced individually and in sequences. Only when such experiences have been assimilated can they be used in relationship with others to effect a total dance experience.

PLATE 59

This illustrates an improvised pair sequence. The boy in front chose to step with a rising movement which became sustained and fine touch in the lift of the head and left arm. The boy following shows active participation as he pays close attention to adapt his movement to that of the leader.

PLATE 60

Here the intention is not to adapt to a leader as in Plate 59 but to work in relationship with a number of others. The boys developed the idea of converging on one individual who sank in the centre. A group feeling was achieved by their ability to fit in around each other. This situation was resolved by a bursting outward initiated by the boy on the ground.

Body part:	"Which part of the body is leading the movement or is mainly active?"
Weight-bearing:	"Are you on one or two feet, high up or near the floor?"
Shape:	"What shape have you arrived in when you stop—spiky, angular, curled up, stretched out, twisted?"

Of the dynamics

Weight:	"Where is the movement strong and energetic, where is it quiet and gentle?"
Time:	"Does the movement get faster and faster and come to a stop, or slow down, or is it a mixture of these?"
Space:	"Do you cut a straight pathway as you make your movement, or do you twist and turn and go in a roundabout way?"

Of the space

Direction:	"Are you following your nose, your ears, your back?"
Levels:	"Are you dancing high, medium or deep? Where do you finish?"
Pathway:	"What pathway are you tracing on the floor? In the air? Angles, curves, twists?"
Extension:	"Are you making big movements, spreading out far, or small near ones?"

Of relationships

In body:	"Are your elbows near to each other, far away? Are your hands touching, above, below each other, one pushing the other one around the other?"
Of people:	"Are you meeting each other, passing by, going together, leading, following?"

The real problem for the teacher of dance, as for the teacher of modern mathematics and science, is to ask the right question at the right time and to ask questions which lead the child to an understanding of the body as a medium of expression. Whatever aspect is being emphasised at any moment, it must be borne in mind that we are concerned with the whole and that the body, its dynamics, its use of space and its relationship to

D

others are always present and involved whether playing a major role or colouring the theme of the sequence or dance. Moreover, the three needs of the child—to explore, to master and to create—are always present. The child in the infant school will be concerned mainly with exploration and creativity and to a lesser extent with mastery. On the other hand, the child in the junior school will be gaining increased mastery but has no less need of opportunities to explore and to create.

CHAPTER 5

Dance in Relation to the other Arts

"Art is deeply involved in the actual process of
perception, thought and bodily action."* *Sir Herbert Read*

As has already been stated in the first chapter, dance can be recognised as the primary art, movement lying at the base of all the other arts. Movement indeed can be considered as an integrating factor in all manifestations of the creative impulse. We have now to consider the relationship between the various art forms and to enquire how far they should deliberately be used as stimuli for each other.

Many authorities have pointed out the difficulty of defining art, but seem to agree that works of art can be recognised. Such works are concerned with man's expression, they are perceived by man's senses and have their own distinctive form and nature. They arise because there appears to be inherent in man a deep desire to express his aspirations, fears, and feelings and to communicate them in works of art.

In writing of the Mawayan and Wai-wai tribes† Nicholas Guppy comments on the way in which these South American Indians, an indigenous population, decorate practically everything they make, including the arrow heads which have such a short life. He observes that all flat surfaces are decorated with painted patterns ranging from semi-naturalistic to abstract, almost geometrical designs. Such work obviously gave pleasure primarily to its creator for it would be seen by few others. In watching these Indians, Nicholas Guppy says that he felt himself close to the origins of artistic creation:

"Creation, therefore, one might define as a form of thinking in which the hands or some other means are used as extensions of the brain, with which to fix images and solve problems—an elaboration in man of the brain's prime role in maintaining the organism in security. And a

* *Education through Art* (Faber & Faber Ltd).   † *Wai-wai* (Penguin Books Ltd).

finished creation is a projection of some part of its creator's inner model of reality, showing the way in which a disturbing feature of the outer world has been incorporated. . . . . For some people, savage or civilised, words or signs provide the imageries most important to them; for others, sounds, shapes, patterns, colours, taste, smells, the sense of touch, physical movements. . . . Individuals may not be able to think at all adequately in any but their special imagery—a painter or mathematician may be incoherent, a writer insensitive to music—yet everyone has to solve problems in his own imagery if he is to maintain his health. . . . Games, gymnastics, the various forms of exhibitionism, shouting, fighting, dancing, sexuality, contain elements of non-verbal thinking so important that mental health may be impaired if they are denied—yet in Western civilisation certain kinds of thinking are so habitually suppressed that they are being systematically evolved out of existence."

Nicholas Guppy shows his considerable insight into the nature and importance of artistic creativity.

The unity of the arts is reflected in the interchangeability of words used to describe them, whether it be the "rise" and "fall" of melody in music, the "tones" in a picture, the "rhythm" in a piece of sculpture, the "angularity" in a dance. Examples of such use of words can be found in any critiques of performances or exhibitions of art.

Thus, for example, in reporting on a performance of Britten's *Cantata Misericordium*, Donald Mitchell writes:

"... there is a tender interior, quality about the invention which is most moving. It is undemonstrative, pure in colour and spare in texture, and all the more affecting just because of its masterly economy. . . . The weight the leading melodic idea of the work accumulates, is astonishing."

Or again, reviewing *The Heart of Artemis* by Bryher, Christopher Wordsworth writes:

"Her book thrums with an almost perilous exultation in travel, experiment, fact, self-knowledge."

In the booklet *Music and Dance in Indian Art*, produced for the Edinburgh

52

Festival, the note about the exhibition of sculpture and models and photographs of temples reads:

"One can certainly say of Indian architecture that it is music in stone. For the whole fabric of an Indian temple is a hugely conceived interplay of rhythms—very complex rhythms. The exterior is covered with mouldings, panels, foliate ornament, little motives, such as small blind arcades, and with sculptures. All are meant to be read crosswise and vertically as rhythms, just like the varied beats of Indian drumming."

Not only do different forms of expression borrow words to describe each other but there are many words which are common to all—balance, harmony, form, symmetry, for example.

A task of the teacher concerned with aesthetic education will be to create situations in which the young child is exposed to many exciting things which will stimulate his senses, inspire and encourage his powers of expression, observation and appreciation in various media. It can be done in many ways. Firstly, the classroom environment itself needs to be exciting and to provide opportunities for children to look, to touch, to listen, to discover. At the simplest level this demands that illustrations, notices, charts and the like must be attractive, tasteful and artistic in themselves and, of course, must be changed frequently. It means that the child must be stimulated constantly by interesting shapes, textures and colours of objects—shells, rocks, tree bark, materials, "junk" which they can both see and handle. It means that he must be introduced to sounds that are unusual—words (sense and nonsense), rhythms of mechanical or electronic origin, sounds of different instruments, improvised sounds, as well as to natural sounds such as birdsong, and music within his range. Such careful observation used in developing the child's awareness and knowledge of the universe is important in the science teaching which has its beginnings in the primary school too.

This experience must not be limited to the classroom but must be extended to the world outside. The child needs to have his attention drawn to the shape, texture and movement of trees, clouds, wind. He can become increasingly sensitive to the sounds, to the happenings, even to the smells of the street, the canal bank, the field, the station, the beach and the rubbish dump. In terms of movement this exposure to a stimulus is used not only when the child observes a tree moving in the wind, or the way in which the speed dies out in a spinning top, but when he responds freely to a rhythm beaten on an instrument or when the teacher makes suggestions which bring him to experience such activities as whirling and spiralling from high to deep; spreading the body wide open and then suddenly gathering it close together again; jumping and leaping through the air.

The child progresses from the simple experiences of listening, touching, doing and, at the junior stage, can become aware of relationship and of the unity in all forms of expression. So, gradually, he can be helped to experience and to appreciate rhythm in his own breathing and heart-beat, in the repeated pattern of a movement with its characteristic stress and relaxation, in a phrase of words, in the repeated shapes in a picture, in a tune played or sung, in the darting of the fish in an aquarium. He should become aware of shape and pattern in a gesture of the hand, in the shape of the body in a position of stillness, in the angular or curved lines of a rock or a shell or a crystal or a piece of sculpture, in the melody of a song, in a formed sentence, in different species of plant life, in wood shavings, flotsam and jetsam. He should become aware of texture in the effort and quality exerted in movement, in the smoothness of clay, or the roughness of bark, in the different sounds of instruments—drum, cymbals, strings—in the weight and feel of a stone or a feather.

As the child becomes aware of these things, he will recognise that in everything there is structure, dynamic potential and shape and that all these are present in an organised fashion in a work of art. This, then, is the task: for the teacher to create an atmosphere in which the child can observe, appreciate and gradually relate experiences so that he becomes aware of the unity from which art springs. This may be termed an "impressive" approach with the stress on exciting and stimulating the senses. To awake and foster the child's senses is, however, not enough. Scope must be given for the feelings, aspirations and moods to find expression in some form in various media, individually and with others. Young children need the opportunity to experiment in all the forms of expression that can be made available and this puts a heavy responsibility upon the teacher. To quote Sir Herbert Read:

"Appreciation, as I have previously emphasised, is not acquired by passive contemplation; we only appreciate beauty on the basis of our own creative aspirations, abortive though these be."

We need then the interplay between the "impressive" and the "expressive." Sometimes one may predominate. The impressions which stimulate a child's experiments in stained glass or modelling clay may last over many practical sessions or days, especially as the actual, created work is there to be returned to and continued. Similarly older juniors may be able to return to a movement invention or dance where they left off, or re-create it together, without much stimulus from the teacher, and go on to complete it. At other times fresh stimulus is needed and in movement lessons this will involve the teacher in bringing the children to experience afresh the rhythms, shapes and relationships which were the basis of their original piece of work.

Perhaps this is an appropriate point to discuss the nature of creativity in dance. On the one hand there is the process, more particularly involved in music, singing and playing instruments, where the child performs something created by someone else and through his own participation and interpretation re-creates it, giving it life and expression, so making it his own. Sometimes in dance, work that appears on the surface to be "imposed" may come into this category. For example, a child may be following his partner in a kind of "follow my leader" phrase of movement. At first it may be a mechanical copying procedure, but as it becomes known and is repeated, and the significance of the movement idea and the relationship is stressed, the movement phrase gains expressive value and the child has, in this way, re-created something which becomes his own. This method, which is in evidence in situations of "following a leader" in pairs or groups, or in performing a study choreographed by the teacher, is used far more extensively in the secondary school than in the primary school. It is, however, one way of increasing the child's vocabulary of movement and helping him to appreciate that there are many ways of fulfilling a given task. It also brings into play his powers of observation, sensitivity and co-operation.

55

On the other hand, in contrast to the "impressive" method of stimulating artistic endeavour, the piece of creative work may be a spontaneous outpouring of the child's need to express himself. In this way he may pick up his brush and paint, may write a description of something that has happened to him, may shape his clay, may take upon himself a character which he acts out, may dance for the very joy of it.

In the infant school this need has largely been catered for by providing opportunities for the free choice of such activities, which at this stage are a form of play. The value of play has been well established by many educationalists.

> "Probably the first form of play in infancy could be called "sense-pleasure" play, revelling in or relishing the experience of movements, pressures, flavours, sounds and so forth."*

Perhaps of all the aspects of expressive play activity to be engaged in freely by the child, movement and dance are the most difficult to cater for since they require space. In some schools opportunities are made to set aside an area, often a corridor, where the children can sometimes have opportunities to dance as a choice of activity. However, in the main and where a large space is available, time is set aside for dance as a class activity. This is even more important than providing individual opportunities in the activity periods, for dance is essentially a shared activity and therefore has a special part to play in education. As a social form of expression dance is valuable in bringing children together.

From the first impressions and stimuli, from the early imaginative strivings and explorations, from the play activities of the infant, there grows at the junior stage a more conscious development of a work of art in which are found attributes fundamental to all the arts.

> "From whatever different sensations the arts may derive, from touch or vision or hearing—on to whatever the artists may project their visions, on statues or murals or melodies—they are one in spirt and meaning. . . . The arts, like gesture and speech, are expressions of man; they confirm and corroborate, in their own individual ways, what their sister arts reflect: man's emotive reaction to stimuli from without and within."†

* Stone and Church.   † "The Commonwealth of Art", Sachs Pub., Dobson.

In painting, modelling and the visual arts the inspiration is given permanent form in material. In music, movement, drama and dance, "matter" is not involved and the impulse to create springs from feeling, mood and the kinaesthetic sense. These art forms are of a transitory nature and have to be recreated whenever they are repeated. While one task is to bring the child to an awareness of unity in created things, another is to make him aware of the particular nature of the medium in which his artistic endeavours may be given expression. This implies a respect for the material to be used and an acceptance of the discipline of the medium.

The child working with paint is concerned with texture and colour and the use of two-dimensional space. In contrast the child working in clay is provided with the opportunity for three-dimensional and plastic expression. When he is exploring the realm of sound he is concerned with pitch, harmony, rhythm. When he is exploring the realm of drama he is concerned with situations, imaginary or realistic, and with human reactions. When he is dancing he is concerned with the flow of action. Whatever medium is used the aim can only be to say what can be said in that medium.

Sir Herbert Read has suggested that from four types of mental function—thinking, feeling, sensation, intuition—are developed four types of artistic style. These are *realism*, art of an imitative nature; *idealism*, art of a spiritual, super-realistic nature; *expressionism*, art of a sensuous nature; and *abstract*, art of cubist type concerned with the forms and qualities of the material. Each of these, he suggests, can be regarded as possessing introvert or extrovert attributes. He further suggests that different aesthetic activities are expressions of the four functions, namely:

Craft	corresponding to	thought
Poetry and drama	corresponding to	feeling
Design	corresponding to	sensation
Music and dance	corresponding to	intuition

In fact it would seem that all these functions are brought into play in every expressive activity and that it is a matter of emphasis rather than selection. Indeed, Read himself says:

"Whenever we speak of a particular type . . . it is not to be assumed that anything more than a predominance . . . is indicated."

The particular nature of the art of movement lies in the fact that all the aspects of the personality are brought into play—body, spirit, intellect, emotions—although certain individuals will stress different ones. It will also be found that types of dance will emphasise particular aspects. Thus a dance may be mainly concerned with bodily technique, may be of a rhythmic or lyrical nature, may be abstract or dramatic in content. Sir Herbert Read takes his thesis further to suggest that different periods in history show a particular preference for one or another type. Thus it would seem that in all forms of contemporary art the emphasis is on the abstract form of expression. Whatever the result—a representational style which gives a pictorial record, an expressionist style which appeals to the senses, an abstract creation which gives pleasure through its inherent forms— whether in paint, stone, music or movement—the main concern should be to give expression to fundamental ideas in a chosen medium.

This was excellently demonstrated by John Berger in a "Monitor" programme on B.B.C. Television in June 1956, in which four pictures of the "Madonna and Child" by Bellini were compared. The first was painted in the 1470's when the artist was forty, and the last in his seventies. The span shows the development of his treatment of light and space from, at first, a two-dimensional point of view in which the observer is outside, through the second painting where the child seems to kick out into space, a third in which the figures face sideways and the shapes are more rounded to a fourth where the figures are in an open field approachable from every direction. In the last the figures are a part of nature in a great volume of space and the Madonna is portrayed without halo. During this period the explorations and discoveries of Columbus, Vasco da Gama and Copernicus were bringing a new awareness of freedom in space!

In the same way Henry Moore is not only concerned with his subjects as such but is exploring the nature of his material and the fundamentals of sculpture: the landscape-like contours, the relationships of shape and space, the ever-changing face as viewed from every side, in varied light, in all weathers, even reflected in water as is his two-piece reclining figure for the Lincoln Centre in New York. In fact he has said that sculpture is purely an interest in form—in shape, not literary ideas.

In the realm of movement this attitude is important. It implies that movement expression may take the form of realism, super-realism, expressionism, abstraction: may be dramatic, lyrical, spatial in stress, but underlying is the exploitation, the exploration, the experience of movement ideas. This is in direct opposition to a view that all art, including dance, must be representational and "tell a story," and is why it is important for the teacher to study and understand the nature of movement itself.

In conclusion, it appears that although the arts have common roots, each one must develop in its own way according to the discipline of its medium. Although it is important to demonstrate the relationship which exists between the many manifestations of the creative impulse, they have independent life and need not always rely on each other for inspiration.

CHAPTER 6

Dance as a Creative Activity

*"The subject matter of dance lies within the verbally almost inaccessible field of vital experiences and qualitative thought." Laban**

HAVING established the fact that the unity of the arts is manifest at a deep rather than a superficial level, it is clear that whenever starting points other than movement are used for a dance, there must be a transmutation into the language of action.

The children cannot "be" wind, water, clouds, but they can take part in such actions as whirling, undulating, waving, rising, sinking, advancing, retreating, gathering, spreading which may be observed in natural phenomena. The children cannot "be" plants and flowers but they can experience a movement phrase developing from a small to a large extension and the gradual process of growth and dying away. The children cannot "be" machines but they can experiment with the repetitive organised actions typical of mechanised operations. Moreover, just as the child using paint or other materials may discover a resemblance to objects in real life, so he may in movement. This is very different from setting the whole class to 'be trees', a misconception about the nature of dance which is still encountered on occasions.

This is not to say that an experience in one artistic, creative activity will not in fact stimulate another. There is plenty of evidence of this type of integrated work in schools. It may take the form of the introduction into a movement lesson of a visual or aural stimulus in order to aid the development of a particular concept. Thus reference may be made in a lesson on turning and spiralling to a paper model of a spiral shape or to work already done in paint or clay. Conversely the movement of such a spiral cut-out placed over the radiator to illustrate the scientific principle of hot air rising may bring forth a suggestion from the children for a movement experience. The point to be emphasised however is that a spiralling up and down is a movement experience and not yet a dance. To create a dance

*Article "Symbol."

the children must experiment to discover the full scope of the movement theme, must select and invent motifs and develop the rhythmic and spatial possibilities. Variations may be made on the original motif or contrast introduced. Thus a spiral upwards could be followed by a simple direct sinking down or vice versa. The size of the pattern could be increased so that a floor pattern would arise. Variations of suddenness and sustainment could be used. Possible relationships with other children in small groups could be explored. Accompaniment might be added. In this way motifs could be developed and a small dance composition created. This is just one example of the way in which a visual stimulus might add to the movement idea and the idea be developed into a dance. The idea has served as a *stimulus*, a starting point, and not become a limitation as can so easily happen.

Sometimes a topic may lend itself to exploration in a number of fields. The topic "Growth and shape in natural phenomena and man's creations" was explored with a class by a group of students and their tutor. Activities which stemmed from it penetrated very different fields. The growth of the City of Worcester was illustrated by reference to the Roman city, the Elizabethan city and present developments. Another group was concerned with the growth of trees into their own particular shapes and, as a more creative activity, with shaping patterns with pressed leaves of varied shapes and colours. Others concentrated on the cycle of the seasons and the colours associated with them and produced creative writing and drama. Yet another group used all sorts of materials to build three-dimensional models, while others developed dance sequences associated with "growth and shape."

Seonaid Robertson illustrates the way in which movement experience and creative writing can be developed from a common theme in her stimulating book, already referred to, which should interest all who are deeply concerned with art education.

A young teacher of nine-year-olds working on the movement theme of elevation found her class so excited and stimulated by the movement experience of jumping and hopping and coming down to earth again, that she gave the children the opportunity of making pictures, where they painted the air pattern of the jumps using appropriate colours, and of writing about the experience. The following poem is one of the results.

JUMPING NICHOLAS HAYES

Twisting and twirling,
Romping and whirling,
Up in the air, down to the floor.
Legs up, hands high,
Straddling and sprawling
Shooting into space
Light as a feather,
Up went I.
Down to the earth
From the sky.

Another teacher working on the theme of near and compact contrasted with wide-spread, large movement developed this in the dance lesson and later in art. In the latter the children found themselves exploring the possibilities of producing solid areas of paint which could be spread out into tentacles over the paper.

With this sort of approach it is clear that it is not a question of dancing a story or painting a dance as much as one of a total experience which permeates many aspects of the child's experience. Such projects cannot easily be carried out by visiting lecturers but are developed by a creative and sensitive teacher. The teacher referred to earlier who had worked on the elevation theme used the story of Noah as a starting point for her class. The following is taken from her written description of the work.

"I played the children the record of the story of 'Noah's Ark.' For the dance I used a tape recording I had made of percussion, part of the *Grand Canyon Suite* and the song from the record. The result was a mixture of dance, dance-drama and mime. The children wrote the story when the dance was well under way. It was written in parts and stimulated by the record, various other pieces of music, and discussion. The result was a story lavishly illustrated in many cases and very much alive as it included recognition of characters and their speech. They included descriptions of the actions of the people and the animals, brought about because they had actually participated in the movement experience. The children painted pictures of the storm and I was anxious that they should be aware in painting of the turbulent movement of the sea and the richness and variety of the colours. I put on 'The Cloudburst' from the *Grand Canyon Suite* while they started to paint. Throughout they did very little talking but were obviously turbulent and could sometimes be observed painting waves with the rhythm of the music. This also had an effect on the dance for, after they had painted it, the whole group of children became much more vigorous in movement in their attack on the ark. The model of the ark was made to scale and we linked it with history. The model also included a landscape and models of men, animals and trees. It was obvious that the model was meaningful, as it was equipped with ingenious ladder arrangements and stones and each morning I would find the animals and people arranged in another activity. I also read to them other flood stories of the same era. Done in this concentric manner one aspect interacted on another."

In developing the theme of "Noah" a topic was chosen which could be explored in a variety of avenues within the whole. It is well to note that it was a suitable theme for such a treatment. In the earlier ideas discussed in this chapter dance was one of several unrelated experiences explored from a common starting point.

There is also the approach in which another art form is used to stimulate dance. Thus texture and colour in a painting may inspire quality in movement; shapes in a sculpture may inspire shaping in movement. As indicated in discussing the use of the visual stimulus of a spiral shape, such starting points have to be developed into dances, unless of course they are used as an additional imaginative aid.

Perhaps the art most allied to dance is music. Like dance its development is concerned with the interweaving of themes and motifs of a rhythmic nature rather than with literal interpretation. Small children will not however be able to dance to long pieces of orchestral or piano music and it is best when using music to choose music for them to use which is short, simple, rhythmically clear and emotionally recognisable. It is a mistake to use too much music. The teacher may expect all the class to conform to the music in a way which allows little scope for individual creativeness. The child will tend to rely on it rather than develop his own rhythms. For these reasons the use of a variety of percussion instruments is the greatest help for sound accompaniment when needed. The use of sound can be a help as an addition to the teacher's words and tone of voice in creating a particular mood. Thus, for example, if the movement experience were to be that of light dancing high into the air contrasted with deep dancing near the ground, the words "light, gentle, airborne" could be supported by shaking bells or light tapping on a tambourine, while the words "strong, energetic, forceful, beating into the ground" could be supported by strong beating of a drum. Accompaniment will also serve to accentuate the rhythm of a movement. In this way it may be used by the teacher to encourage a rhythmic activity. It may be used by the child as he is dancing so that he creates a dance phrase and accompaniment at one and the same time. It may serve as a unifying agent for a group of children working together. It may be introduced as the final stage to accompany a dance created first of all in movement. School percussion instruments such as castanets, triangles and tambourines can be used and children can make their own improvised instruments but it is advisable to collect together a number of instruments of really good quality and tone. This would include a large cymbal, a good tambourine and a tunable tambor. Instruments from abroad if obtainable such as wooden xylophones, Chinese or African drums and temple blocks are valuable additions.

Apart from responding to music and using percussion, children will readily use their own voices. Infants spontaneously make their own noises to accompany actions. They will also pick up and repeat words or sounds used by the teacher. Juniors too will seize opportunities to make their own voice accompaniments. While referring to the use of sound it is important to stress the need for movement to develop independently of sound. Individual children can then create their own movement rhythms and phrases. Children in the top class of the junior school have proved themselves capable of developing group motifs based on effort rhythms where the rhythmic content is brought out solely in the movement.

It remains to discuss the use of stories as starting points for dance. It is widely believed that this is an easy "way in" to dance for beginners. In fact it needs considerable knowledge of movement to transmute stories into movement and considerable skill in selecting suitable stories and poems. The teacher must be aware that whenever literary ideas are used the movement which results will tend to be a dramatic representation. This will be a perfectly valid experience but it differs from the rhythmic flow of action and themes interweaving that constitutes a dance. Dance will more easily be experienced through the use and development of movement ideas. Dance lies not in the realm of imaginary situations and the interplay of characters but in the total personal involvement in action and movement experience and for this reason it has its own special part to play in the child's education.

Index

Abstract, 57, 58, 59
Action, 18, 60, 65
Accompaniment, 35, 37, 38, 42, 44, 45, 61, 64
Air pattern, 24
"Arrow-like" body shape, 21, 45
Art of Movement, 17–18
Arts, the, 11, 14, 16, 18, 51–59
Asymmetry, 20, 38, 45

"Ball-like" body shape, 21, 45
Bodily action, 11, 16, 43
Body activities, 19, 33, 48
    awareness, 33, 34, 36, 37, 40, 44
    flow, 21, 38, 45
    parts 20, 33, 34, 49
    shape, 18, 21, 37, 38, 40, 44, 45, 49
Bound flow, 22, 36
Bruner, Jerome S., 14, 15, 16

Colour, 17, 53, 61, 63
Craft, 57
Creativity, 15, 17, 42, 48, 50, 51–52, 54

Dab, 22, 41
Dance, 11, 44, 57, 59
Dance sequences, 38, 42, 47, 48, 61
    composition, 48, 55, 61
Design, 57
Direction in space, 23, 40, 49
Directness, 22, 38, 39
Discovery, 15, 16, 17, 32, 53
Door plane, 23
Drama, 11, 13, 57
Dynamics, 18, 49

Effort, 16, 19, 44, 45, 46
Effort actions, 40, 46
    qualities, 33, 34, 36, 37, 38–39
    rhythm, 40, 64
    transitions, 40
Elevation, 19–20, 33, 34, 37, 61
Extension in space, 22, 23, 49
Experiment, 31–32, 54
Expressionism, 57, 59

Fine touch, 22, 36, 37, 39
Firmness, 22, 36, 37, 39
Flexibility, 22, 38
Flick, 22, 41, 47
Float, 22, 41, 47
Flow, 22, 36
Free flow, 22, 36, 45

Gesture, 20, 37
Group relationships, 38, 42
    rhythms, 46
    sequences, 40, 46
    shape, 40
Guppy Nicholas, 51–52

Idealism, 57
Infant themes, 33–35
Intuition, 15, 17
Invention, 17, 48

Junior themes, 35–42

Kinaesthetic sense, 13, 18, 57

Laban, Rudolf, 15, 16, 29, 31, 32, 43, 60
Learning Process, 14–17, 31
Level, 23, 35, 40, 44, 49
Literature, 16, 64–65
Locomotion, 19, 33, 34

Moore, Henry, 58
Movement as a means of expression, 11–14, 16
    ideas, 32, 43, 49
    mastery, 17, 30
    memory, 42, 48
    observation, 18, 28, 29, 43
    themes, 16, 30, 31
    vocabulary, 29, 53
Music, 57, 63

Painting, 13, 14, 58, 61, 63
Phrasing, 35
Play, 56
Poetry, 57, 62

Press, 22, 41, 47
Primary School, 11, 18
Punch, 22, 40, 46

Read, Sir H., 51, 57–58
Realism, 57, 59
Relationship, 18, 19, 25, 34, 35, 36, 40, 42, 44, 45, 46, 49
Rhythm, 12, 16, 18, 40, 46, 54, 64
Robertson, Seonaid M., 13, 61

Sachs, Curt, 56
Sculpture, 13, 57, 58, 63
"Screw-like" body shape, 21, 45
Shape, 18, 19, 21, 53, 54
Slash, 22, 41
Sound, 13, 18, 53, 54, 64
Space, 19, 23–25, 33, 35, 49
Space awareness, 23–25, 41, 44
    pathways, 35, 36, 40, 42, 49
    patterns, 24–25, 36

Speed, 33, 34
Spontaneity, 12, 56
Stimulus, 51, 53–54, 60
Suddenness, 22, 34, 36, 37, 39, 44, 45
Sustainment, 22, 34, 36, 37, 39, 44, 45
Symmetry, 20, 38, 45

Table plane, 24
Texture, 17, 18, 53, 54, 63
Thrust, 22, 40, 46
Time, 22, 34, 36, 49

Visual Arts, 51–53, 57

"Wall-like" body shape, 21
Weight, 22, 33, 34, 36, 49
Wheel plane, 24
Word Suggestions, 64
Wring, 22, 41